MADE WITH TOUGHLOVE

Real Life Business Stories

TOUGHLOVE ADVISORS

PASSIONPRENEUR®
PUBLISHING

Made with TOUGHLOVE
Copyright © 2023 TOUGHLOVE Advisors
First published in 2023

Print: 978-1-76124-077-5
E-book: 978-1-76124-078-2
Hardback: 978-1-76124-079-9

Because of the dynamic nature of the Internet, any web addresses or links contained in this book may have changed since publication and may no longer be valid. The information in this book is based on the author's experiences and opinions. The views expressed in this book are solely those of the author and do not necessarily reflect the views of the publisher; the publisher hereby disclaims any responsibility for them.

The author of this book does not dispense any form of medical, legal, financial, or technical advice either directly or indirectly. The intent of the author is solely to provide information of a general nature to help you in your quest for personal development and growth. In the event you use any of the information in this book, the author and the publisher assume no responsibility for your actions. If any form of expert assistance is required, the services of a competent professional should be sought.

Publishing information
Publishing and design facilitated by Passionpreneur Publishing
A division of Passionpreneur Organization Pty Ltd
ABN: 48640637529

Melbourne, VIC | Australia
www.passionpreneurpublishing.com

To our friends, colleagues, managers, teachers, partners, spouses, and family members who gave us Tough Love over the years to help us learn and grow, both as individuals and professionals.

TABLE OF CONTENTS

ACKNOWLEDGMENTS

We are thrilled that this book is in your hands. Our deepest hope is that it serves you and enables you to unleash your potential. We think this book is special because it brings together nine authors who come from different backgrounds to share lessons and experiences from their own perspectives.

Tough Love is an age-old concept and aspect of human behaviour. It tends to be practised haphazardly and reactively. We thought we would re-package it and allow our readers to get a taste of how potent it can be when properly harnessed.

This is the product of our experiences – and how enriched they have been by the people we have encountered on our journeys. Along the way we've had supporters to whom we shall be eternally grateful and – importantly – we have had our fair share of critics who have served us some really tough love. To them we owe a debt we can never repay.

To our colleagues, friends, managers, clients, suppliers, mentors and coaches, we say THANK YOU, and we commit to paying it forward. We are not mentioning anyone by name, because with nine of us, we might need an additional chapter to include everyone. You know who you are.

We would also like to express our thanks and sincere appreciation to our spouses and partners who stood by us, supported us and gave us some real Tough Love when we most needed it throughout our careers – and from the day we came together to form TOUGHLOVE Advisors.

INTRODUCTION

*'RECOGNIZE THAT TOUGH LOVE IS BOTH
THE HARDEST AND THE MOST IMPORTANT
TYPE OF LOVE TO GIVE (BECAUSE IT IS
SO RARELY WELCOMED).'*

— RAY DALIO

Tough Love is not for everyone, nor is this book, because we did not set out to write another book filled with theory or political correctness. We say it as it is; we share our knowledge gained from triumphs and failures in life and business – with our gloves off, as is the case in our daily practice at TOUGHLOVE Advisors.

The title of the book, *Made with Tough Love*, is self-explanatory. That spirit is built into every chapter of this book. They include an account of how the TOUGHLOVE squad of nine came together, and many real-life experiences, personal stories and examples about critical topics that can make or break an organisation.

This book covers numerous topics: leadership, the 101 of brand experience, the importance of organisational culture, the anatomy of marketing, what it takes to stay in the game with digital transformation, how to innovate in an ever-changing world – and we even explore where the world is going with the Metaverse. What more could you want?

This also means you don't have to buy several books to be inspired to improve your business, learn something new or get better at your job.

As Ray Dalio suggests in the above quote, Tough Love is hard to give and sometimes even harder to receive, but we know that in the end it is well worth it.

To give Tough Love:

Is the willingness to apply one's learning from mistakes in the interest of helping others achieve growth and progress.

To receive Tough Love:

Is the willingness to receive unfiltered, straight-talking advice from someone whose only interest is to help co-create a solution.

Each chapter of this book is written by a different author/ partner of TOUGHLOVE Advisors, on a topic that is close to their heart and in their area of expertise. Accordingly, each chapter has its own style and approach. You will meet a variety of authentic voices speaking from different experiences in different industries – from Aviation, Banking, Advertising, Cosmetics, Packaging, Food and Beverage, Oil and Gas, Technology and Telecommunication.

Another beauty of this book is that its authors come from nine different backgrounds and nationalities – American, Canadian, Lebanese, Saudi, Bahraini, English, Greek, Turkish and Indian.

Are you ready for some Tough Love?

The TOUGHLOVE Story

Let me start by telling you the story behind TOUGHLOVE, how the idea came about, and how we came together to form a dream team, a disruptive and awesome company named TOUGHLOVE Advisors.

08:30 AM, LAUSANNE, SWITZERLAND

On a typical cold and crisp Swiss January morning in 2017, I was briskly walking along lake Leman from my hotel to the company's head office and enjoying the view of the snow-covered mountains. The lake was calm, the breeze on my face was refreshing, and the sun was peaking from behind the many cotton clouds, typically Swiss. Many thoughts and questions were running through my head.

'I wonder how the day will go ... what they'll recommend ... what will be decided ... how many people will be impacted ... and how much will we save?' At the same time, I was thinking 'I am so hungry ... I hope we'll have those crispy warm Swiss croissants at the meeting.'

As I reached the office reception, which was stark and intimidating, I removed my rarely used winter coat and walked quickly to the main conference room, early enough to secure a good seat next to someone I liked. I saw some familiar faces and some new ones. They all had the same sober look, in anticipation of the long and tough day ahead. I said my good morning in the three languages spoken by the people there: 'Good morning, Bonjour and Buongiorno'.

The room was too hot. Water and fruit had been placed in the centre of the long table, which had wires everywhere powering the many laptops scattered about. One side of the conference room had a long transparent glass wall that magically became frosted at the push of a button. The other side had that beautiful view of the lake and snow-covered mountains – a little distracting at times, but certainly better than being in a room with four gloomy walls.

This was the usual head office meeting, where we discussed company strategy, objectives and plans, led by our friendly consultants who were commissioned to lead this 'right-sizing' or restructuring project.

The consultants were suited and booted and had a pompous air about them. They introduced themselves unenthusiastically, and we did the same. Although there were some familiar faces around the table, we all then introduced ourselves as if it were the first time.

I remember catching myself responding to emails and exchanging WhatsApp messages during the early part of the meeting. I was bored and couldn't engage. The presentation already seemed long; lots of new terminologies were introduced, with jargon words flying around the room as if trying to impress each other. They made one sound smart, but the truth is, none of us understood what they really meant.

At one point, I remember noticing the number on the bottom of the slide we were looking at … it was slide 57. I wondered: how many more slides will we see today?

(Just a side note before I continue, if you have a long presentation to share, which I never recommend, please don't use slide numbers. They only remind your audience of how much time you've stolen from their lives.)

The meeting continued until about 17:00, interrupted by lunch and a couple of coffee breaks, and by then 197 slides had been bestowed upon us, of which I could only remember about four or five. I thought they might be useful to add to my own presentation, which was scheduled for the following week.

Several of us decided to walk back to the hotel together. We exchanged thoughts and reflections about the meeting and the value we felt we took from it.

A couple of my colleagues thought the session was interesting but far too long for what was relevant and useful. I thought that there was a lot of repetition and a plethora of theory; I was convinced that we could have spent half a day on the subject and still walked away with the same information.

One of my colleagues said, 'But they have to justify their fees. I heard this project is costing us in excess of €1 million.'

'Wow,' I thought to myself, 'When I grow up, I want to be a consultant.'

My reflections on that meeting stayed with me for quite some time. I wondered if there was a better way to do these things. Could people benefit from an independent advisor who would bring in relevant and valuable outside views? There are two distinct reasons that I ask this question.

First, when you are entrenched in the corporate world for many years, working for one big multinational company complete with its own ecosystem, you tend to forget that there is a world out there.

The second reason is a little more sensitive. You can find yourself recommending a course of action for months, to address a certain challenge or solve a specific problem, yet no one is listening to you or your proposals. Perhaps it's because they think you may have your own agenda, or worse, they may not think you are qualified enough to make those recommendations. Then some outside person comes trotting in on a white horse with the same recommendation dressed up in jargon and a confetti shower of theory and everyone gobbles it up.

Fast forward to mid-August 2021.

11:00 AM, DUBAI, UAE

I had just returned to hot and steaming Dubai from my annual summer family vacation in Canada and was getting myself mentally prepared for the autumn season and the usual business cycle that comes with it. Lots of management meetings, budget reviews and planning, headcount and people review discussions, setting agendas, reviewing activities and campaigns for the balance of the year.

I was sitting in my home office that morning when I received a phone call from a colleague to say there were signs of another restructuring in the company.

'Ok,' I thought. 'Covid-19 has played havoc with several factors, from the cost of raw materials to logistical delays. There have been challenges creating significant impact on margins in our company, and every other industry, for that matter.'

My initial thought was 'If this change is going to impact my position, that's ok. If I don't leave now, then when? I have been in the company for 20 years and in the corporate world for over 30, and this could be an opportunity for me to do something new.'

I started to have flashbacks from all my years of experiences, from the places I've been and the people I've met and learnt from. All were incredible and valuable memories, but the ones that stuck with me the most were the points in my life when I learnt something new. Something that shook me – 'aha' moments, comments and feedback that shaped me and made me reflect.

One such moment occurred in my late thirties, when my boss at that time, who I knew secretly liked me and appreciated what I did, asked me if he could give me some 'tough love'. He proceeded to give me some brutally honest feedback about my presentation style. He asked if I could take this feedback, sleep on it, and come back and present to him again the next day – and the next day – until it had sunk in and I felt comfortable with my new way of presenting.

He said that I spoke too fast and without pauses, neither allowing the audience to understand my message nor giving them time to reflect on what I had just said; he said that I fidgeted too much on stage, distracting people from the message I was trying to convey. I remember he used the term 'pregnant pauses'. I had to learn what that meant and how important they were to any speech or presentation. He also said that some of my slides were too busy for anyone to follow, that the audience didn't know whether to read my busy slides or listen to my 'Speedy Gonzales' presentation style.

At the beginning of the feedback process, I was a little uncomfortable, maybe a little embarrassed. I didn't know how to take it. Should I be offended? Demotivated? But I quickly realised that he wanted the best for me, especially when he offered to take the time to coach me.

That stuck with me, and so did the term he used, 'tough love'. From that point onwards, I practised that technique and approach with colleagues and people I cared about, especially the ones I saw potential in.

Back to August 2021. By the end of the month it was confirmed that my role was impacted by the restructuring and that no other option was on the cards in the company because I didn't want to leave Dubai, the city I felt married to.

I had mixed feelings at first, in one way I was sad to leave a company I helped build for over 20 years, and in another I was relieved. More importantly, I was excited about what I could now do – armed with the knowledge and experience I had gained about discipline, compliance, matrix organisations, managing people, managing a function, and all the good things that come with it.

A new life began for me on that day.

But before I take you forward, let me take you back to 4 April 2016. That was when, along with a couple of my business partners, I was exhibiting our social media start-up at The Step Conference 2016. The start-up was initially called 'My-Sign' and later launched as 1TAM (1 Thing About Me). 1TAM was the first ever UAE Vlogging App – it was almost exactly like TikTok today but without the multimillion-dollar funding. I can vividly remember the number of hours, nights and weekends I spent with my two partners, Anwar Nusseibeh and Jean Philippe Roth.

That day, I was talking to our French developers, who'd flown in from France, and some other visitors to our miniature start-up stand who were interested in the idea behind our App. Then from the back of the hall, a balding English gentleman, whom I would dub a professional connector, approached me to say hello. I recognized him; it was James Welch, the man I had contacted via email a couple of weeks before to help us market the App.

He was full of energy and spoke a mile a minute. We chatted for a while. I told him about our App, what problems it intended to solve and all the features it had. At the end of the conversation, he paused, smiled and asked me if I would like to join the board of something that was being formed in Dubai at the time called 'The Marketing Society'. I remember him saying 'Because you are an extraordinarily busy guy, I think you would be a great fit.'

He was right, I was extremely busy juggling my full-time day job in a multinational company and establishing a couple of start-ups and investing in others. I had co-founded and led 1TAM. I had invested in a Swedish organic drinks company called 'Caliente' and an American tyre recycling company called 'Green Source Holdings'. I had become a shareholder in a Lebanese start-up bank called Cedrus, which went from an investment bank to a retail bank. Thankfully, my wife put up with me and my constant buzzing between meetings and initiatives and did not run for the hills.

I thought, what the heck, The Marketing Society sounded like an interesting opportunity to network and learn, but even more valuable were the other interesting people on the board. They were the CMOs of every global and regional brand being represented in the region.

I joined the board of The Marketing Society in 2016, at a time when there were fewer than 100 members. In August 2018, I became the Chairman of the Marketing Society in the UAE, which is a global community of leading marketers from the world's best brands.

I share this story with you to put into context how my involvement with The Marketing Society influenced the birth of TOUGHLOVE.

Ok, let's jump back to 2021. I had been meeting with and keeping an eye on different people in and outside of The Marketing Society to help me bring the idea of TOUGHLOVE to life.

This idea had been simmering inside my head for years, but I wasn't sure when to start. The idea was to form a power-house of practitioners – strong enough to power a nuclear plant – to come together as a squad to help companies and leaders with their business, strategy, marketing, and growth challenges. We would be straight talkers, telling people what they need to hear to solve problems – not what they *want*ed to hear. We would use as little jargon as possible (which I had become allergic to); we would use our experience to engage in real conversations, not PowerPoint slides or theories. In other words, the intention was to disrupt the traditional consulting model.

Let me share with you how I met and brought together the squad of eight people who are now the co-founders of TOUGHLOVE.

Kamal Dimachkie is a soft-spoken man, as fit as an athlete, who tends to think a couple of times before he utters a word. He is a leader, a strategist, and a communicator. He has spent over three decades in advertising in the region and around the world, and he is considered a living legend in that industry.

We met for lunch one day in Media City in Dubai, and he shared with me his plans, in confidence, that after 33 years with Publicis Group and Leo Burnett, he was stepping down from his Chief Operating Officer position. I was trying to recruit him to join the board of The Marketing Society (and succeeded, by the way), but a couple of other bells rang in my head. He could be a part of the squad.

Tim Burnell is an English gentleman, and I mean that in every sense of the word. I used to hear about him in different circles but never had the opportunity to meet him. He liked to make himself scarce. I invited him to my office – the clubhouse of the Emirates Golf Club, where I play golf – to learn more about him and his plans. It was a meeting of the minds: we both come from a Comms and brand-centric background; we speak the same language and know the same circles. Tim spent about three decades working for Emirates Airlines, First Abu Dhabi Bank (the largest bank in the Middle East) and Etihad Airways in senior roles.

Tim speaks purposefully and eloquently, with a posh English accent. He is either so well dressed that you wonder if he's just returned from a GQ shoot, or he comes dressed in casual shorts and a T-shirt – nothing in the middle.

Then there is Mohammed Ismaeel Hameedaldin, and Mohammed here is with a double 'm' – more on that later. The first time I met Mohammed properly was when I presented him with the Marketer of the Year award. He had certainly earned it as a key player and maker and shaker in the marketing scene in the region. I remember him telling me that he doesn't really like the limelight and tends to avoid it when possible.

Mohammed was invited to join the board of The Marketing Society and later became the chairman of the Society's Dubai hub, whilst being the CMO for Visa in the EMEA region. So, in short, we became a notch above acquaintances. We would meet at different meetings and occasions, and I would tell Mohammed about my plans for TOUGHLOVE. I remember him smirking throughout my spiel every time.

I later found out why. He said that everything I told him about my experiences and plans for TOUGHLOVE felt and sounded as if I were talking about him – or reading his thoughts. Mohammed is a Saudi citizen with Royal Yemeni roots who speaks with a perfect English accent. He comes across as a well-travelled diplomat, but what is more remarkable about Mohammed is that he is an accomplished marketer who has done the rounds of just about every global brand – Citibank, Proctor and Gamble, HSBC, and Visa, just to name a few. I have met no one who doesn't know Mohammed and doesn't speak highly of him.

Yes, we do have another Mohamed on our team, and this is Mohamed Al Tajer, with one 'm'. Mohamed and I became social media friends before we met in person. He was stuck in another country, whilst his family was in Dubai, and he wanted to explore ideas and opportunities that would unite him with his family. When we finally met, it was an instant connection. We spoke the same language, had a similar outlook on business and life, and we both wanted to do something to give back, rather than pursue another corporate career.

I met Mohamed in person for the first time at my office at the clubhouse and learned about an impressive career spanning more than 30 years with brands like Wrigley, Coca-Cola, Gulf Air, Majed Al Futtaim, Citigroup, National Bank of Kuwait, Qatar National Bank and more. Mohamed is a man with endless energy and an incredible ability to connect anything or anyone. He reminds me of the slogan for the Energizer Bunny commercial – he 'keeps going and going …'

I first met Eddie Maalouf through a very dear friend, Ghassan Khoury. When Ghassan introduced the two of us years back, he said, 'I think you'll like this guy because he is a pragmatic, no-nonsense, accomplished businessman and an absolute gem of a person.' During our first meeting, I was attracted to his brutal honesty when giving an opinion about a topic or a person, and he would selectively spice his candid opinions.

We attempted to meet and catch up for years, but we were both very busy with work and travel, so we never got the chance until he joined a customer of my ex-company, and I had the chance to connect and reignite that friendship-in-waiting.

Eddie is a well-known figure in the telecom industry. He led Nokia's growth in the region when Nokia was the king and queen of the mobile handset revolution. He is also an ad man who has led or managed several global ad agencies in the region; he has also built and sold one. Surprisingly, he is a photojournalist by training. He speaks Spanish fluently and is exceptionally good with numbers … especially when you start negotiating with him.

He can come across as a man with a constant frown, which can be a bit intimidating, but this man has a heart of gold.

I remember being at a fast-paced business event in downtown Dubai. I was preparing to start the evening proceedings when a distinct accent caught my attention. I had lived in Istanbul for four years and that English with a Turkish flavour was unmistakable. I moved closer to the group and introduced myself to Nurcin Erdogan. 'Any relation?', I asked when she had told me her name. She said 'no' with a half-smile. The evening ended successfully, and I rushed back home, without getting a chance to talk to her again.

A couple of days later, Nurcin and I met again at a major event at Dubai World Trade Centre called 'Marketing Mania'. The Marketing Society had a full-day agenda, and I was chairing the day. During the break, Nurcin and I talked about what she was doing and about her past experiences. I learnt that before moving to Dubai she had lived and worked in Shanghai with her family for four years, and her career spanned positions with various global brands like Logitech, DAN, Red Bull, BAT and L'Oréal.

Nurcin is a determined character who talks with conviction and passion about whatever she is interested in. When I spoke about the concept of TOUGHLOVE, she listened for a while and then started to give me her opinion about it by drawing some diagrams, lines, and circles on her iPad.

I knew that if Nurcin joined our team she would bring a diverse point of view, along with knowledge and experience in branding and people and culture. So, I invited her to meet the other partners for their input and agreement, which she instantly received.

From that point onwards, I was not the only one interviewing for partners. We decided that bringing in the right people was an extremely important ingredient to our success. Experience and talent were of course a given, but even more important was chemistry and fit with the team. Luckily the original squad instantly gelled and the chemistry was off the charts.

We knew that the business world – commerce, strategy, product management, retail, advertising, communication, marketing, and everything in between – had changed exponentially since Covid, especially in the areas of digital innovation and transformation. So, with that need backdrop, we focused our search on people who have led digital transformation initiatives and were strong in that skill set.

A couple of days later, Mohamed (one 'm'), forwarded me a message from a LinkedIn contact of his enquiring about collaboration opportunities. She knew nothing about TOUGHLOVE, and it was a pure coincidence that she possessed exactly what we were looking for in a digitally savvy partner.

We decided to invite Namrata Balwani to meet both Mohamed and me. From that first meeting, I knew there was something there, but I couldn't put my finger on it. Namrata comes across as a little timid and quiet, but that is just for show. In fact, I remember her once saying to me, 'Don't let my soft and quiet demeanour fool you.' We later found that to be true; Namrata is a feisty and opinionated person when the rubber hits the road. She co-founded an independent digital marketing agency called 'Media2win', was a regional unit head for Ogilvy One in India and then moved to Dubai to lead a digital transformation initiative for the largest retailer group in the Middle East.

Namrata had to endure five different rounds of interviews, in different locations around the city and with multiple questions from different partners. She certainly had her share, too, of provocative questions, which made us realise that we needed to sharpen some pencils. Regardless, she remained interested and committed to joining the team and being part of our journey.

Kamal and I usually have a weekly one-on-one catch-up meeting at 'the office', our base at one of the outlets of the Emirates Golf Club (EGC), or over the phone. We don't have fancy offices with mahogany-clad walls, leather chairs or chicly designed reception areas, so we don't charge our clients for these costs. With minimum overheads, our costs are focused on our billable hours.

But I digress. My meetings with Kamal usually concern new ideas about the structure of the company and reflections on progress. One point we often discussed is how we make decisions. Minor and operational decisions are made by me as the CEO and our Executive Team, as relevant, whilst major decisions are made through a partners' vote, with each partner getting one vote. This ensures engagement and empowerment of the partner team – but it could also slow us down and encourage politics amongst us in the case of split decisions.

This potential bottleneck made us decide to bring in a ninth partner.

The search began again, but this time with a specific skill requirement for someone with digital innovation and transformation experience. We knew we had a powerhouse in

Namrata, but we expected a lot of clients to have this kind of need and wanted to make sure we would not be spread too thinly.

Mohammed was having lunch one day with an ex-colleague of his, spreading the word about TOUGHLOVE. Eleni Kitra listened intently and asked a lot of questions. Mohammed came back saying Eleni herself might be interested. I wasn't surprised that she would like our concept, but I was surprised that she would be interested in joining, as she had a full-time and very demanding senior management role at Facebook (Meta).

We agreed that we would leave it until she came back from a business trip to clarify her level of interest. We were certainly interested in having Eleni and her vast experience, industry knowledge and reputation on our team, but we were not accepting part-time partners.

Each partner accepted, as part of our shareholder agreement, to dedicate as much time as possible for TOUGHLOVE, whether selling our services or delivering on client projects. Partners can also pursue multiple other businesses and opportunities as long as they don't have any conflict of interest with what TOUGHLOVE is offering.

Our first meeting with Eleni was also at 'the office', with three other partners and me. We told her what we were planning and how far along we were. We answered the questions Eleni had, and she had plenty. She was excited and energised about the idea, even though she had just flown in on an overnight flight.

She talked about her interests and career, which has spanned over 30 years working for global companies like Sony, MultiChoice Group and OMD before joining Facebook. What we learnt is that Eleni had the same mid-career itch we did and was clear that she wanted to step down from corporate and start something of her own. She even had the timeline set and had talked about it with her family.

What a coincidence, I thought. Good for Eleni and awesome for us.

We agreed we would reflect on the discussion and the opportunity and regroup with the balance of the partner team. Two days later I received a phone call whilst playing golf on the Faldo course at Emirates Golf Club (EGC). It was built in 1988 as the first grass golf course in the Middle East, back when Dubai was a simple port city with huge ambitions. The call was from Eleni, expressing interest in joining our team and playing an integral part in the company's growth.

So we were nine.

A week or so later, we were at my house celebrating the official launch of TOUGHLOVE. Some of us joined remotely via zoom, as they were quarantining due to close contact with Covid cases.

Early on, we agreed that TOUGHLOVE was the master brand and that all our various services would be under that name. We established TOUGHLOVE Advisors, which is the primary sub-brand, TOUGHLOVE Podcasts, TOUGHLOVE Talks, TOUGHLOVE Learning and Development, and TOUGHLOVE Board, through which companies can benefit from the experience of having a non-executive board member from TOUGHLOVE on their board.

After many discussions and self-evaluation, we decided to offer five different areas of advisory service. Each area would be called a Practice Pillar. In simple terms, and without boring you with the details (also mentioned on our amazing website, https://toughloveadvisors.com), these five areas are:

1. **Strategy and Management,** covering, corporate vision and purpose, long-term growth strategy, business planning and change management.
2. **People and Culture,** which includes culture design, employee experience and engagement, organisational design and restructure, and talent management.
3. **Business Operations and Performance,** which involves new market entry, growth and portfolio management, channel strategy and RTM, and demand generation.
4. **Digital Transformation and Business Innovation,** which concerns digital transformation, immersive experiences, innovation strategies and c-commerce and e-commerce.
5. **Brand Marketing** and **Marketing Communications,** which involves many areas, such as brand positioning and

identity, brand campaign development, research and consumer insights, communication planning and marketing operations.

Phew! That was a bit of a spiel, but it is important to emphasize that we are a multidisciplinary advisory, not just Marketing and Communications, as some initially perceived us. I have often heard the remark, 'Oh, so you do more than branding, marketing, and Comms-related advisory?'

To have an arrangement like this – a group of high-powered people who have had armies reporting to them but are now on a team of equals – we had to establish some rules and agree on some values. From the first meeting, the concept of TOUGHLOVE has been to provide a service that is simple and practical, has value for money and is jargon free. We knew that was what potential customers wanted because we have been on the 'other' side and that is what is most lacking.

We agreed on our company values in the same spirit. TOUGHLOVE's values are:

Candour: Positive, constructive and caring candour, with each other and with our clients. It is the cornerstone of what Tough Love is all about.

Trust: Trusting each other and seeking to earn our clients' trust. Without trust, tough love will be misunderstood.

Agility: Our USP is in how we deliver our services and in our decision-making processes. Agility is more attitude than process, more environment than methodology.

Simplicity: We don't like or talk jargon. We present our ideas and recommendations in simple and easy-to-understand language to solve customers' problems.

The first two values focus on how we behave with each other and with our clients. The second two focus on how we conduct our business. I subscribe to Albert Einstein's way of thinking: 'Everything should be made as simple as possible, but no simpler'.

Every time I think of our TOUGHLOVE team and what we can deliver as value to our clients, as well as what we can achieve together, I am super excited. My excitement comes from the energy and the spirit behind the team's coming together. It also comes from the experience and maturity they bring to the TOUGHLOVE table – and how our lucky clients will benefit from them.

No matter what happens, and where TOUGHLOVE goes from here, I wanted to keep a souvenir of this special achievement, as well as give the business community a glimpse of what experience and professionalism look like. So, we decided to write this book together, each contributing a chapter.

What you are about to read are the nine TOUGHLOVE steps to drive personal and professional growth. We hope you enjoy this book and, most importantly, gain benefit for your personal and professional development and growth.

In the spirit of candour and transparency, I want to come clean and reveal that putting together a book by nine different, and very busy, contributors was no easy feat. Comparing it to 'pulling teeth' would be an understatement.

Everyone needs some TOUGHLOVE sometimes. Enjoy.

ABOUT THE AUTHOR:
KHALED ISMAIL

CEO/Partner

Khaled is a pragmatic business leader who is fascinated by businesses and their inner workings. He is a former global executive leading Marketing, Branding, Public Affairs and Communications operations for Europe, Central Asia, and the Middle East and Africa Region.

He has more than 30 years' experience, beginning in advertising and continuing in international sales, marketing and branding in FMCG (B2C) and the Food Packaging Industries (B2B), including Tetra Pak and The Coca-Cola Company.

Khaled has a Bachelor of Commerce degree from Concordia University (Canada) and has completed several executive programmes in leadership and management at Ashridge (UK), IMD (Switzerland) and the Harvard Business School (USA).

He is an active investor in technology, beverages, sports marketing and finance. Born in Beirut, Khaled is a Canadian citizen; he has lived and worked in 15 countries and now calls Dubai home.

Khaled is also the Chairman of the Marketing Society-UAE and is a very well-respected business leader, public speaker, marketer and mentor to young entrepreneurs.

Khaled is a published author of a book titled *This Is What Tickles Me.*

The Fourth Kind of Horse

Developing Leadership – The Path to Mastery

KAMAL DIMACHKIE

LOVE AT FIRST SIGHT

S heltered from the Lebanese Civil War, in the Lebanese Chouf Mountains, my school provided what in retrospect feels like an idyllic environment for a teenager to grow up in. There was fresh air, plenty of physical activity, a huge plot of land over which the campus spread, and a wonderful mix of people who came, as tends to be the case over there, from a multitude of social backgrounds. We studied hard, played hard, and had plenty of freedom to roam the grounds.

It was a cool Saturday morning when the boarding school supervisor summoned us to the football pitch. Boys and girls of different ages, we wondered why we were there and eagerly awaited the reveal. In struts a beautiful grey mare full of energy, yet with one of the kindest expressions I had ever seen. One by one, we were helped onto her back and led in a small circle. I had no riding experience whatsoever but was instantly smitten and felt something stir inside me. It was love at first sight!

With hindsight, I now better understand my reaction – getting hooked was coupled with a determination to become good at something. At first a fleeting thought, it gathered momentum and scale. It was a revealing moment about how I would come to react to things I was determined to master.

My recollection of the rest of that morning is hazy, but I taught myself how to ride, and I remember well the speed with which my bond with horses grew. I invested time and effort and had fun along the way. Weeks gave way to months and before the year was out, I had become a capable rider, very comfortable in the saddle. Little did I know how big a role riding and horses would play in my life, or the attachment I would develop for beast and sport.

FOUR KINDS OF HORSES

Fast forward to 1988, as I was being groomed to take on the leadership of the Procter & Gamble account for the Leo Burnett agency in the Middle East-North Africa region. To help mentor me, my then boss shared many articles with me; in one of them I read the following quote from Shunryu Suzuki, which has stuck with me:

> It is said that there are four kinds of horses: excellent ones, good ones, poor ones, and bad ones. The best horse will run slow and fast, right and left, at the driver's will, before it sees the shadow of the whip; the second best will run as

well as the first one does, just before the whip reaches its skin; the third one will run when it feels pain on its body; the fourth will run after the pain penetrates to the marrow of its bones. You can imagine how difficult it is for the fourth one to learn how to run!

We all want to be the first kind of horse, and why not? It is smart, it moves intuitively, and it displays a strong bond with its rider. What we might miss from this story is that it is the fourth kind of horse, not the first, that displays the ability to learn. Ultimately, pain and discomfort are part of the learning process, and what we need along the way in life is to be able to learn and grow from experiences.

At times, I have felt that this was written for me; I identified with this analogy of the horses, and I certainly made sure never to lose it along the way.

A NOT SO OBVIOUS PATH

Commit to remarkable

I was fortunate to have been thrust into positions of leadership early in my life and career, but my journey along that path was anything but linear. My professional life has been rife with mistakes and a lack of awareness. It was torturous, circuitous, and so painful that I have often referred to myself as **the fourth kind of horse**.

Driven by a determination to achieve, to honour obligations and rise to the occasion, my approach has at times been abrasive and insensitive; I have even followed a scorched earth policy, leaving devastation in its wake. I obtained results, but at what cost?

Like a tone-deaf person, I often missed the signals. The environment around us is rich with cues! Whether we pick them up is another matter, and I certainly took my sweet time about it. People's reactions to my actions and words were signals that I often missed. I missed them because I wasn't paying attention – I was focused on driving projects, meeting deadlines, and enabling my clients to succeed. I was raising the standard, representing my agency and ensuring that when a mistake was committed, we learned from it and did not repeat it. My heart was in the right place, but the path I seem to have chosen was not the most effective and productive one.

In an environment that idolised success and frowned upon failure, I felt an unequivocal drive to succeed and excel. Sadly, there was no room in such a period for reflection and consideration. Coaching was unheard of, and mentorship was hard to come by – especially when my first boss was relocated six months into my assignment. I found myself on my own and needing to chart a course whose success or failure had implications for the wider agency. Once again, and without realising it, I found myself needing to become self-taught – as it had been in riding, so too in business and dealing with people.

Deep inside, I knew that there was more to what was happening; it was as if I could hear a faint knocking on doors all around me but wasn't sure how to open them. That got me thinking.

PATTERNS EMERGE

Embrace the journey of self-discovery

Time on the plateau is an invaluable gift! This is the time of repeating actions and tasks over and over until we can replicate them fluently and reflexively. Conventional wisdom pushes us to reject the plateau and to seek the ascent, to climb and scale. Make no mistake, I am all for climbing and scaling heights and summits, but my love is reserved for the plateau, for making the effort, for embracing the discipline and tirelessness of repeating until it becomes natural. It all started with the thought that there had to be a better way.

Weeks gave way to months, and months to years; what emerged were patterns of thought and behaviour that became impossible to miss. The plateau allowed me to experiment and repeat, to observe and refine, to fail and rise again, to try, to miss, but to remain undeterred in moving forward in a journey of learning.

As we seek to improve, it often feels as if life wants us to be sure of what we want. We don't get results quickly. It is as if the door we are banging on sort of asks you: 'Are you sure of what you are doing? Are you sure you want it answered? If so, keep on knocking and knock louder.' What that meant was that my journey did not unfold along a straight line, it meandered like a path in the forest. There have been starts and stops, trial and error, and iteration. My footsteps weren't always sure; there was hesitation, there was second-guessing, there was plenty of doubt and a lot of fear –sentiments often exacerbated with failed attempts.

There was no surprise in any of that. How could there have been when there was no roadmap or blueprint for what I was attempting to discover and address? It was an excruciatingly slow process unfolding over time in all its units, small and large, from minutes and hours to months and years.

The lesson was one of self-discovery, and that means that my journey, like everyone's journey, is singular and unique. It moved at a pace specific to me. Admittedly, life has been generous, for the signals were all around me: the reactions of others, both encouraging and disparaging; the things I succeeded at and those I didn't; the joy others experienced while collaborating with me and the dejection some felt after a particular interaction. At times, feedback came gently – at others very bluntly.

Self-awareness may come more easily to some than to others. I am not sure where I fit, assuming there is a spectrum. However, if you seek, you shall find. It became increasingly clear that, as Marcus Aurelius famously said, 'The mind adapts and converts to its own purposes the obstacle to our acting. The impediment to action advances action. What stands in the way becomes the way.' Ultimately, the obstacle becomes the way, and that was me, the obstacle being my own behaviour, my own thoughts, my own assumptions.

I changed tack. Rather than start from a thought and allow it to dictate behaviour, I started from the behaviour that was blocking me. I anchored it as a destination I did not desire to manifest. With effort and steadfastness, that reverse engineering started paying off. Clarity about what behaviour I did *not* want forced a sense of calmness that permeated my mind and elicited a different thought, which in turn produced a different outcome.

THE PENNY DROPS

Don't underestimate the power of small changes

I cannot think of a specific moment when the bulb lit! As I think about it, I came to that realisation with hindsight, after many attempts, mixed results, and sustained disappointment followed by plenty of time to reflect. Throughout, the question 'What is it that I want?' kept materialising for me. It begged an answer, and my curiosity demanded satisfaction.

It didn't really feel like I was climbing stairs; it was more like walking up a ramp. Meanwhile, slowly yet surely, gently, change took place. It was akin to water carving stone through repeated dripping, one gentle drop at a time until, over time, the rock was carved and became smooth.

Behavioural shifts took place one experience at a time. With every interaction, the reactions of my counterparts helped me refine and polish who I was. I seemed to be operating on missile lock, my mind firmly fixed on a desired quality of outcome, and my entire being had to deliver on it. Over time, my responsibilities grew and that meant that I had more and more people to look after and lead. I took this responsibility seriously, felt a strong obligation to model the way and to ensure that I provided a good example.

People are interesting in the sense that they are always watching you and reconciling word with deed. What you claim and do say a great deal about you; people may like and agree with you or dislike and disagree with you. However, they will certainly keep score when what you claim is not delivered upon in your dealings with them. People are watching, so when there is a lack of congruence, this is when they will react and share their views; some will do so constructively, others less so and yet another group may choose to quietly disagree and show through their behaviour that they are not fans. We all have a choice to make, and in my case, I took the approach of taking all in, sometimes with great difficulty and begrudgingly, and used such signals as springboards for further improvement.

BREAKING THROUGH THE CHRYSALIS

Be relentless

In the beginning desired results are infrequent, sporadic; yet scattered examples confirm their existence and the possibility of delivering more. With repetition and commitment, I realised, these were pillars upon which I could raise a structure. Once again, that demanded a commitment to the plateau. Mr Miyagi of *The Karate Kid* fame encouraged Daniel-san to 'Wax in, wax out' until his hands and wrists were sore. What Daniel-san did not realise is that through repetition one builds reflexes and muscles. Through repetition and a commitment to the plateau, one builds strength.

There is truth to what Marcus Aurelius said. The caterpillar's transformation is not complete until it metamorphoses and breaks through the chrysalis. Only when it is strong enough and has developed into this beautiful, strong-winged butterfly can it break through; its only way out is to penetrate through the walls of the chrysalis that holds it. The obstacle is the way.

I knew I was on to something when I saw those who interacted with me come to new awareness, when their lives, careers, and ways of being evolved for the better, and when the impact my interactions produced helped them move forward, develop, and grow into better versions of themselves. That realisation produced joy and made me want to produce more of it, not because of selfish pleasure and satisfaction but for the betterment of others, the propagation of best practice and the elevation of the profession and the person.

Something was happening to me. A metamorphosis was on the way, and while I never thought of myself as a leader, the fact that I repeatedly found myself leading through adversity started connecting dots; it started to show me that I could lead others to success, achievement, and growth.

I found myself going against the grain. Where others enjoyed the shortcut, I enjoyed the long way and made it my friend. Where others shunned difficulty and wanted a quick result, I relished the effort. Others hated adversity, but I knew that it was my best friend and that it polishes the soul.

Effort, sweat, hard work, resilience and mastery became cool and sexy. It took me forever to realise that, but there is something inspiring in coming from far behind in life, from growing through adversity, from repeatedly hitting the wall and then becoming a standard setter. I didn't figure it out quickly, but others' reactions to me changed.

If there was a leader all along in the chrysalis, I never knew it. I realised that as I stepped forward, took charge, and committed, energy was spread to those around me, and with it came the belief that we can do remarkable things and achieve. Progressively, the reactions of others around me told me what I never saw for myself and claimed. A leader was in the making.

TO LEAD. TO INSPIRE.

Inspire and breed respect

As a private man in a public industry, I got to observe quite a bit. I watched others around me and made mental notes. There were many examples to follow and many more to avoid. Some provided inspiration, others raised red flags; all provided me with material from which to learn. I find leaders and people in positions of authority to be fascinating creatures, and I often wonder if they are aware of what they are communicating all along.

Growing up and spending most of my life in the Middle East provided me with many examples of how people throw their weight around; how power emanates from the top and trickles down; how it is used; how some justify their actions, thinking that providing justification upfront excuses behaviour; how many rule by fiat and how they allow ego to sit in the driver's seat.

I watched all this with fascination and resolved never to be that kind of leader. I had, and continue to have, a very different kind of image in my mind. For me, it has always been abundantly clear that there is only one form of leadership … leadership by example. Don't get me wrong, other forms may exist, but only one is sustainable. The rest are like physically abusing your body, or the environment, and expecting the bill never to come due. There shall always be a reckoning.

My choices have nothing to do with fear but with inspiration and light. Unless you are prepared to walk the talk, then no matter how high up in the organisation you reach, you lose the moral right to lead and drive. You see, one's behaviour, decisions, and conduct (how they show up, how they model, whether they are self-serving or not) must be able to breed respect. Remember that … *breed respect.*

Ultimately, leadership is about being Gandhian in being, in thought, and in conduct. This means that one needs to be the change they want to see around them. You want people to show up on time – start by being first in the room; you want your people to work late because it is required – avoid the excuses and be in the trenches with them; stay late. You want those around you to excel – set a high standard for yourself and your output that will make them want to achieve it and beat it.

My people deserved a good example, and I was determined to provide it. Clearly, I wasn't a master of everything, but there were things I was particularly good at, and I helped those around me to become good at them too. Along the way, it became clear that discipline and hard work were not the enemies of creativity. Inspiration creates joy and builds drive, and guess what happens as a result? People thrive, they succeed, and they grow.

A LONG JOURNEY

Be a missionary, not a mercenary

As a child, I watched the world around me, and that observation started at home. I was clear on what I did not want, and I filled the years between then and today with hard work and dedication. I showed up every day no matter how bad things were, and at times they were quite bad. On the days when I could not progress, I tried to make sure not to regress unless there was a strategic reason why. I seem to have decided to take charge and responsibility for my life and its outcomes.

From an early age, I had to shoulder responsibility, I had to work, I had to make sacrifices – the kind that burn – and accept trade-offs, some of which were not particularly pleasant. In hindsight, I consider myself lucky, as it taught me from early on to appreciate the joy of discipline and hard work.

Today, I can take some pride in having properly done what I have been entrusted to do, to have pushed the boundaries, to have built a foundation of success for those around me and those above me, and to have properly and honourably represented the organisations to which I have belonged.

I am far from done as I change tack in my life and move on to more challenging endeavours. I am thrilled to have carved time to give back to a variety of organisations and causes, not least of which is my academic involvement as I support students in the field of innovation and entrepreneurship, women's empowerment, and environmental protection. I continue to write and speak publicly whenever the opportunity arises. I also continue to learn and broaden my knowledge and skill base.

If you observe nature, you may notice that all living things grow. Things that don't grow are not alive. To be alive, one must continue to grow, not just in years but in the mind.

TAKING PRIDE

Go for impact

As a leader, the thing you take pride in is not what you have achieved, your status, the money you made or your possessions. The thing that a leader takes pride in is the impact they have had on the people whose lives they touched.

It is said that a pebble never knows the impact it leaves on the surface of a pond, and like that pebble, I shall never know what impact I may have had on the lives of people around me. However, as I look around me at some of those with whom I have worked and see what heights they have scaled and how they have built their lives – compared with where they have come from – that is when I allow myself a moment to celebrate the privilege of their touching my life and I theirs.

There are a few examples of such individuals who have gone on to lead organisations, to build new offerings, to thrive and, each in their own style, to model the way. In so doing, they are propagating the practice of leadership and they inspire as they create impact.

I am delighted and truly humbled by seeing them do so.

LEADERSHIP WITHOUT SHORTCUTS

There is no recipe or secret sauce that I can recommend. Ultimately, each leader's journey is individual and unique and certainly shaped by the circumstances around them. I am of the view that there are some principles that can help keep us on the path. These are mine:

- **Commit to remarkable.** In a world and an era where every single one of our needs has been catered for many times over, the way forward is not through more of the same, not through safe recipes and not through treading water. We need to create value and make an impact, and that can only be done by being remarkable. This requires risk-taking, daring, courage and accepting that success may be elusive but not if we keep trying. While you are at it, do something remarkable, because anything short of that doesn't cut it anymore.
- **Insist on the highest of standards.** This means preparation, anticipation, and attention to detail. It also means both demanding more of yourself – and doing it before you make demands on those around you.
- **Have backbone; disagree and commit.** Life is a contact sport of people and ideas, and it is nourished by

continuous healthy and, at times, animated debate. This requires people to speak up and speak the truth, especially to power. It is a matter of integrity and transparency that involves the right to dissent. But, in the end and once a decision is made, commit.

- **Be a missionary, not a mercenary.** Both will hold a job, get paid, and perhaps get tasks done; only one fuels the soul of the endeavour they are engaged in.
- **Be relentless.** Relentless is good. It is tireless and unyielding, producing results, and it is inspiring. Relentless is what we need today, tomorrow and way into the future.
- **Have empathy.** It is said that everyone you meet is fighting a fight you know nothing about. Be kind! Be empathetic and understanding, so you can help people achieve their potential – as a result, the community may attain its own potential.
- **Inspire.** The true test of leadership does not come when the sailing is smooth; it comes during adversity. When we fare rough seas the need to be a cheerleader is paramount and requires disproportionate effort. It doesn't mean that you cannot and shouldn't serve tough love, but inspiration is about pointing the way forward and shining a light.

AND ...

The world may be reeling today and trying to adjust its thinking from abundance to scarcity, but there can never be enough leaders. There is an obvious need for leaders who inspire, who give their people a larger-than-life purpose for the work they do. As a leader, your mission is to help develop, build, and enable the people around you to deliver remarkable things. In so doing they will create opportunity, generate growth and build success, and this drives prosperity.

And leadership is messy, organic; it isn't straightforward, and there is no silver bullet for it or secret sauce. It is individual, personal, contextual and fallible. This is what makes it so magical and achievable. To be a leader, one must inspire, as opposed to driving by fear and fiat. To do so, a leader must commit to the path of lifelong learning and humility. So, the next time you are tempted to order people about, walk a mile in their shoes before you ask them to walk a mile in yours.

ABOUT THE AUTHOR:
KAMAL DIMACHKIE

COO/Partner

A versatile leader and a polyvalent talent, Kamal is the COO and co-founder of TOUGHLOVE Advisors, and the former COO of Publicis Communications and Leo Burnett UAE, Kuwait, and the Lower Gulf.

With 40+ years of experience spanning the MENA region and North America, Kamal brings considerable expertise and a solid track record of leading teams and developing people, managing complexity, inspiring creative development, and delivering against growth targets.

Kamal has also served as an adjunct instructor in integrated marketing communications at the American University of Dubai. He is an ex-board member at the IAA UAE Chapter and currently sits on the board of The Marketing Society.

As part of giving back, Kamal serves as a coach for Endeavor and a mentor with Cartier Women's Initiative, supporting women entrepreneurs. He is also a non-executive Board Advisor with Sacred Groves.

He holds a B.Sc. and an MBA from the American University of Beirut and has recently earned an ACTP certificate from the University of Texas at Dallas Executive & Professional Coaching Program and an ACC certification from the ICF.

Culture Eats Strategy for Breakfast, Lunch and Dinner?

The Invisible Force that Makes or Breaks It for Many Businesses

NURCIN ERDOGAN LOFFLER

*PEOPLE WILL FORGET WHAT YOU SAID,
PEOPLE WILL FORGET WHAT YOU DID, BUT
PEOPLE WILL NEVER FORGET HOW YOU
MADE THEM FEEL.*

— MAYA ANGELOU

In the 20+ years that I have been in business, for the majority of the companies I worked for and for the majority of the people I worked with, work sucked. I have met hundreds of intelligent, well-educated people who were drained and overwhelmed by unreasonable demands, tired of office politics, cursing it and craving the weekend. Funnily enough, it never mattered what their level of seniority was or what kind of package they had. The majority were suffering in the workplace and openly saying the culture they were working in was 'toxic'.

Did you know that the average person spends 90,000 hours at work over a lifetime? 90,000 unhappy hours of being unproductive, unengaged, uncreative. 90,000 hours when their full potential is being wasted. 90,000 hours in an environment that is 'toxic' – imagine the impact that makes on one's life.

This is not acceptable. How on earth could we not be doing something to change this? This realisation has become the core of my journey to understand and design human experiences and cultures that allow people to flourish.

I knew I was obsessed with making sense of human behaviour early in my life, and that has not changed during my career. When I studied psychology and topped it up with a Marketing MA, my vision was that marketing is social psychology; it was all about creating perceptions in the human mind through understanding the deeper needs of human beings. Through that journey, focusing on consumers, seeing the internal struggles of successful brands, I realised it was time for me to close that circle and bring the same mindset inside. Brand marketing is creating a change in the outside world, and brand culture is doing the inner work. It has extreme benefits for the people, for the business and for the end consumers. This is because extraordinary, successful brands are created within, through their people.

By the end of this chapter, you'll be able to understand what culture is, how it works, and more importantly, what it is *not*. There are many misconceptions around culture that take away so much from businesses and from people's experiences. I hope this chapter will enable you to better understand how

CULTURE EATS STRATEGY FOR BREAKFAST, LUNCH AND DINNER?

culture design works. I hope it will motivate you to make a difference for your people and leverage your culture for better business results.

EVERY BUSINESS IS A HUMAN BUSINESS: UNDERSTANDING THE HUMAN MIND AND ITS CONNECTION TO CULTURE

Before we attempt to understand what culture in an organisation is, we need to prepare ourselves to take a deep dive into the human mind. It is indeed a common practice in business life to think of structures, org charts, consumers, microsegments, tags, and cookies. As marketers or leaders, we tend to forget that in the end we are all human, and all levels of business are levels of human business.

Shall we conduct a fun experiment together?

Imagine you have decided to go to an all-night party. You have three big boxes with air holes punched into them.

In the first box, you place your pet gecko with some water.

In the second, you put your pet dog with some water and their favourite treats.

And in the third box, you place your spouse or life partner with water and their favourite sweets.

Then you go out and party all night. Let's imagine how each of these creatures would welcome you when you return and open the boxes.

The gecko will probably look at you uncomprehendingly and stay in the box. As geckos don't have a limbic brain (holding some of our memories and emotions), your presence and absence might not make a big difference to this pet. On the other hand, your dog will probably jump up and down with the same happiness and joy they always experience when they see you. Your spouse or partner will probably not be at all pleased. They might take the opportunity to remember everything you have done wrong in the last 20 years, determined to make you serve your sentence. I will leave the rest to your imagination.

The point is that the human mind is complex and sophisticated. The interaction between our thoughts, the language we use, the beliefs we develop, the emotions we feel, and the visualisation power we have is what makes us very special. It's the unique formation of the human mind that drives us to innovate, desire, and progress. But at the same time, it leaves us very vulnerable when our needs are not met. We need to bear this in mind when we think about culture, organisational effectiveness and employee engagement.

THE 'E' WORD

What do you think is one of the biggest insults in professional life? I think it is the 'E' word. Bear with me; you'll know what I mean when I tell you the following story. It's true, and it happened about a decade ago.

It's that time of the month, the day of the board meeting. Every department has a maximum of 20 minutes to present. The pressure is high, your results can get you support, praise, even a higher budget – or get you smashed, as you see the thing you have been working on for weeks be declined.

The board members are lined up with their expensive cookies and coffees, ready for an intense all-day meeting, some already looking tired and bored at 9 am. Most department heads have not had enough sleep; they've been up discussing the details of their 15-slide presentations.

And the show begins.

I was brand new in the organisation, which allowed me to be the fly on the wall and witness the collective norms, or what I like to call the 'how we do things here' of the company. The country head of one of the critical markets was to present the next six months' plans, including a new product launch. I think I don't even need to say that there were not many other women at the table.

Three slides into her presentation, the dominant market lead cuts her off, and with a sarcastic tone asks, 'will it be as successful as the previous launch plan of yours?'. Then comes an awkward silence for two seconds, which feels a lot longer than that. I know nothing of what they are speaking about – but it smells like baggage. I can observe how the presenter is triggered. I can hear the silent laughter in the room. This so-called joke is what I equate to a nuclear attack in a cold war. Of course, the presenter's attitude becomes sour, and she adds a few defensive statements about how underserved her team is and how hard they work.

When she leaves the room, the man next to me leans toward the man who made the 'joke' and says with his eyes rolling, 'She is always so emotional,' and everyone on that table sits silently in agreement, nodding heads with a nasty smirk on their faces.

No one reflects on the attack made on her at the start of her presentation or that she might feel threatened to be the only woman country lead; instead, they choose only to notice her reaction and call her 'emotional'. At an unspoken level, they all agree that women are emotional and dramatic; hence there has never been, and never will be a woman business lead at their so-called 'table'.

The 'E' word in business is 'emotional'. Trust me, it's way worse than the 'F' word. Many mean and inappropriate words and attitudes can be acceptable, yet for some weird reason, at some point, it was decided that getting emotional, having feelings or showing vulnerability is not acceptable in the workplace. And it's even trickier for a woman, especially a leader, to show or share emotion.

There are so many alarming things about this story. And sadly, it repeats itself; continents, countries, and companies change, but this story remains the same.

The key question is, what will we do about it?

We are emotional beings (unlike the gecko we have a limbic system!) and without learning how to use emotions and understand what they really are, we are just in denial and ignorance in the workplace. We are blindly promoting a lack of emotional intelligence, hiding behind armour, yet still seeing significant damage. There is a cost to ignoring emotions.

DECONSTRUCTING LANGUAGE, EMOTIONS AND EMOTIONAL INTELLIGENCE AT WORK

Julio Ollala, who is the President of the Newfield Network,[1] a consulting company and coaching school, says (and I agree) that language is action. Moods and emotions are predispositions to action. I think the story I just shared is a great example to understand how braided these concepts are. They are inseparable, sometimes to the point that they become invisible. We can sense the mood in a meeting room, but we can't necessarily name what is different about it.

---

1   https://www.ncbi.nlm.nih.gov/pmc/articles/PMC4685518/

To expand our understanding of cultures, we need to create awareness of this cycle, welcoming emotions and understanding that they have a lot to do with human behaviour, and breaking patterns on linguistic and emotional levels. Doing so will influence both individual and collective human behaviour.

OUR NEEDS DEFINE OUR EXPERIENCES, PERCEPTIONS AND REACTIONS

Unless we understand the human mind, how our beliefs are formed, and how our behaviours and emotions are affected by them and by one another, we will only ever be scratching the surface of things around culture. Every attempt to fix the culture will just be re-painting a building about to collapse.

The existence of cultures mainly comes from the fact that humans are social beings who cannot exist independently. We have to be in social settings; we have to be with each other. That surely applies to the corporate world as well; we rely on a social structure for the work to get done. To design the culture that will work for our company and brand the best, we need to understand underlying needs. Only by doing so can we prepare the ground for a great culture that will manifest incredible results.

To start with, to function at higher levels and excel, the human mind first needs to assure survival. Survival, by definition, has evolved as we have evolved. We are no longer worried about being eaten by a lion, but now we need to feel a different kind of safety. We need to feel safe and secure even to turn on anything related to our prefrontal cortex, which controls wise decisions, creativity, empathy, and everything necessary for outstanding business results.

If we are in the zone of 'It's not safe here, and I need to protect myself from danger,' it is impossible to see the big picture and find any meaning in our work.

Lack of safety and trust is also one of the primary triggers of the sort of burnout cases that have been occurred so frequently in the last years. The stress hormone that should be turned on and off for only short periods instead stays on for months and years, taking a toll on our mental wellbeing, not to mention our productivity.

When I mention safety and security, it's not only job security I am referring to, but also, and perhaps more importantly, psychological safety. Psychological safety refers to an individual's perception of the consequences of taking an interpersonal risk. It is also a shared belief that a team is safe to take risks in the face of being seen as ignorant, incompetent, negative, or disruptive. In teams with high psychological safety, teammates feel safe to take risks around their team members. They feel confident that no one on the team will embarrass or punish anyone else for admitting a mistake, asking a question, or offering a new idea.

Google's five-year study on highly productive teams, Project Aristotle, found that psychological safety – team members feeling safe to take risks and be vulnerable in front of each other – was 'far and away the most important of the five dynamics that set successful teams apart'.[2] The researchers found that what really matters is less to do with who is on a team, and more about how the team works together.

For humans to flourish, once our need for safety and security is established, we need a sense of belonging. Our reliance on our group members has profoundly influenced our motivation: successful group functioning requires that we are motivated to interact and engage with those around us. In other words, we need to belong.[3]

What do people mean when they say they talk about a sense of 'belonging' at their jobs? Belonging does not necessarily mean being popular with colleagues, nor does it mean feeling connected with work peers because you attended the same schools or live in the same neighbourhoods.

In her 2017 book, *Braving the Wilderness*, Brene Brown share this definition:

> *True belonging is the spiritual practice of believing in and belonging to yourself so deeply that you can share your most authentic self with the world and find sacredness in both being a part of something and standing alone in the wilderness.*

---

2   https://rework.withgoogle.com/print/guides/5721312655835136/
3   https://coqual.org/

True belonging doesn't require you to change who you are; it requires you to *be* who you are.

The greatest barrier to true belonging is fitting in or changing who we are so we can be accepted. When we create a culture of fitting in and seeking approval at work, we are not only stifling individuality – we are also inhibiting people's sense of true belonging. People desperately want to be part of something, and they want to experience profound connection with others, but they don't want to sacrifice their authenticity, freedom, or power to be a part of something and find meaning in it.

Building on belonging is self-actualisation: this is when people start caring about their individual contribution and recognition. Our work and craft are great sources of fulfilment for our need for progress. We feel fulfilled through our contribution, and when we know our contribution is recognised and appreciated, we commit. Then the belonging becomes even stronger; we start to be emotionally invested in our brand.

On the top of the pyramid is purpose, and we see that personal purpose becomes stronger with brand purpose. For people to find their purpose and bring it to work, it's essential that the first three base needs are fundamentally met: safety, belonging and self-actualization. That's what we need to know about the human mind and its needs if we intend to build a meaningful work culture that will bring out everyone's A-game.

TOUGHLOVE CULTURE MODEL

BRAND ACTUALIZATION

PURPOSE
VALUES
INNOVATION

SELF ACTUALIZATION

AUTONOMY,
PROGRESS,
RECOGNITION,
LEADERSHIP

RELATIONSHIPS

BELONGING,
BELIEFS, RITUALS, ENGAGEMENT,
EXPERIENCE

**CULTURE
FOUNDATION**

TRUST / SAFETY / FAIRNESS
WELL - BEING & RESILIENCE
RULES & REGULATIONS
PROCESSES & PRINCIPLES

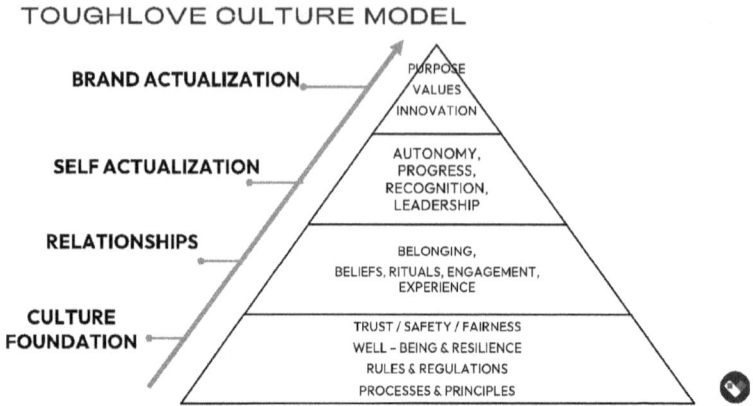

DIAGRAM: TOUGHLOVE CULTURE MODEL

WHAT IS CULTURE?

Culture is the collective programming of the mind that distinguishes the members of one group or category of people from another.

In its simplest form, culture is 'how we do things here'.

Even before we dive into organisational culture, or brand culture as I like to call it, we can observe the complex yet very powerful dynamics of culture in the world we live in and the families we are born into. We human beings, being social and emotional beings, have developed unspoken rules.

IT STARTS WITH THE LEADER AND IS EXECUTED BY THE MANY

I was two months into a new role in a new company, after being reviewed by three assessment centres, cases and many interviews; it had doubled my package and offered me a very exciting title and scope of responsibilities. The offices were in every design and business magazine you could ever imagine. Abundance was an understatement. Free drinks, free lunch, the coolest office design, game room, recreation room, library, movies, each meeting room designed based on a legendary movie star...

Being 5–6 years into my professional life, the day I signed the offer letter was the day I determined in my mind that this was the company in which I would blossom for many years to come. But reality turned out to be different from what I expected, and it had everything to do with culture.

It definitely was a rough start. The cultural cues spoke louder than words, and they were everywhere from day one. As a newcomer, we all go through reprogramming our minds to internalise the collective norms in the first months. For me, every interaction felt like hitting my head against a wall. Even simple email exchanges gave me anxiety, as the communication style they used was foreign to me and left me confused, if not lost. Even the people in my own team barely responded to my questions; some did not even respond at all.

When it was time to go to one of the biggest resorts in the country for the yearly kick-off, I was excited. I thought to myself, 'Great, now the ice will be broken. I will have the chance to meet the regional heads in person and show them how passionate I am to help their business.' I even thought to myself, 'I know, with the spark in my eyes, I can win them over' – spoiler alert: that's not what happened.

It was that moment, when the leader of the organisation took the stage, that it occurred to me. Imagine a dark room, filled with more than 1000 employees (where maybe only 10 per cent are women) with a leader on the stage, shouting at the top of his lungs as if we were all in a scene from *Braveheart*.

Already drenched in sweat, and with a serious emotional investment: 'Are we gonna bury them alive?' (Them being the biggest competition) – the crowd responds in a wild scream 'Yeahhhhh!'

The leader goes on: 'Are we gonna beat them badly?' – the crowd screams 'Yeaaaah!'

This rather wild and to me violent exchange felt like it went for several hours, but it probably was not that long. That evening, when I went to bed, I could not fall asleep. I stared at the ceiling and thought to myself, 'Oops'.

The rest of my two years in that company were challenging but there were no surprises once I decoded the culture. Everything and every day was about 'beating each other' in that culture. There was a latent and inexplicable rage, which took such a toll on the productivity and the quality of the work.

I'm not saying being competitive as a company is wrong. What I want to showcase is that the attitude of the leader sets the tone for the whole organisation. It starts with the leader, goes full circle and ends with the leader. And that attitude has real-life consequences for the work and for everyone involved in that business.

SUB-CULTURES: THE INDUSTRY, BRAND AND CUSTOMERS ARE DIRECTLY LINKED TO DEFINING THE RIGHT CULTURE

Let me share another story from the earliest days of my career. When I first graduated, I started working for my dream company, one of the biggest cosmetic companies in the world, with a very diverse range of brands and products. They had four main business lines, and even though it was all around personal care and cosmetics, the sales channels, positionings, and industries these brands targeted were completely different.

Located in of the coolest districts of Istanbul, they had one big building consisting of four floors. Each floor was dedicated to one of the four divisions: the professional division; the pharmacy division, with derma-focused products; the luxury division that did business with luxury and boutique department stores; and the consumer division, which focused on the FMCG channel.

I realised that, in the same company, one big brand lived with four completely different cultures. Even though there was a seamless sense of community and overarching purpose, the sub-cultures were distinctly different and shaped by the nature of their business.

When I started in the professional division, responsible for professional hair care and technical products, I had no idea what to expect. I was simply happy, thinking that I would be in a great office, wearing high heels and doing fancy and important (!) things. Once the initial boarding was completed, I showed up in the office at 7 am, ready to rock and roll my Ally Mcbeal-style office life. I quickly realised that our floor would not have anyone arriving before 9:30 am, and even then, they would take their sweet time kissing one another on the cheek and having loooong, looong morning chats before they got on with work.

I was labelled as the cold newbie because I was not kissing everyone good morning, nor was my chit-chat up to par. And if my memory serves me right, it took me a good couple of months before I could figure out how to communicate with the team, as well as our clients (and trust me, that was weird even for those pre-Covid days).

This group of marketers was directly working with hairdressers, who are extremely relationship-based decision-makers. They value long-term partnerships; they consider themselves artists and will prioritise personal preferences for a team from a brand over the commercial or technical benefits. They needed to be adored and pampered by their business partners. And this was one hundred per cent replicated in the sub-culture the team lived in.

On the other hand, the luxury floor, which was working on the high-end brands, would always be cold and distant, were always judging every other department, even as they were having their own internal drama.

The FMCG floor, where they worked on fast-moving self-care products, was hardcore trade and business. They were very meticulous about meeting timings; their pace and dynamics were completely different. People did show up at 7 am and had to work a lot longer hours with a different kind of dynamism.

Having had the chance to work across these floors, it became apparent to me that the sub-cultures within a single organisation and/or the larger culture of any organisation have to be linked to its business universe. It's the same for any brand; hence there is not and will never be one culture that fits all. There is no good culture that will work for everyone.

Later, when I started working on brand positioning and culture design, I realised that the link between these two concepts tends to remain under the radar. The service industry, B2B brands, sports brands – they all have to reflect the customer experience through employee experience.

ERASE THE VALUES FROM THE WALL, RATHER BRING THEM TO LIFE

I walked into the office of a big automotive company to have a meeting with the CEO on their culture transformation. The global HQ knew they were in big trouble when it came to their culture and, not surprisingly everything around that – business results, employer branding, brand value in the minds of their customers – started being affected by it. It was only then that they seemed to recognise that an internal change needed to happen first.

The regional CEO was worried that the global team's push for culture transformation would not be relevant to the local markets. This topic could be a book on its own. There is so much to think about when it comes to big MNCs trying to build a brand culture while considering the different cultures in which they need to co-exist.

One of the key topics we were discussing was the need to make sure values are deeply understood and internalized. The HR head said confidently, 'Everyone knows our values; this effort would be a waste of time.'

I asked, 'Do they really, really know?'. He said, 'It's written on the wall of the entrance, and every screen in the building shows them on loop – they have to know.' At that moment, I decided to take the risk and challenge him: 'Shall we just go out and ask the three people we come across right now?' – and we did.

No one could tell us more than two of the nouns that made up the so-called values, found on the wall and on screens. But this was not even the problem. The ones who recalled the values had no idea what they meant for them in their daily lives.

The receptionist who was sitting in front of the screen that showed values all day could indeed repeat most of the nouns, but when I asked her 'what does it mean to be innovative for you every day?', she looked at me with blank eyes and said, 'I am a receptionist, not an engineer.'

And that right there is the biggest problem both with how we approach values when building culture and how we act on values when creating culture transformation programs. The values that define our culture have to be verbs – not nouns. They have to be accessible enough for everyone to understand how to behave and how not to act.

I can ask you this question: how can a receptionist be innovative? The one I asked didn't know. She thought innovation was for scientists and engineers. But suppose the value was 'We solve problems at hand with creative solutions'? That would work for the scientist and the receptionist on a daily basis. And this is what makes the difference.

In everything to do with work culture, we need to make sure to translate values from concepts to behaviours, from nouns to verbs. Also, we need to show how a given value is relevant for everyone, regardless of their level in the organisation.

Otherwise, values become a source of exclusion. To build the culture, we need to equip our people with the skills they need to show up in a way that's aligned with those values. Only then can we create a culture in which we hold one another accountable for staying aligned with the identified values.

MYTHS AND BIG MISTAKES ABOUT CULTURE

Before I wrap up this chapter, I would like to share some comments I have received from leaders. There are many misconceptions about what culture is. Even when intentions are good, I find these misconceptions very dangerous, as they can keep leaders from taking the right actions.

#1 Giving perks, yoga classes, or free lunches is culture.

This is a big misconception, probably the most common one. As Silicon Valley companies become famous for their perks, there is a growing belief among leaders that perks result in the desired culture. This could not be further from the truth.

I'm not saying that companies should not do yoga classes – they definitely should invest in and encourage their employees' physical and mental wellbeing. It's a great initiative, yet alone, it is not enough to give a company a strong culture. Leaders experience disappointment that teams are still not happy and engaged; such extrinsic motivation factors do not last long enough to instil a collective behavioural change nor bring happiness or gratitude to individuals.

#2 Culture is not our priority this year; we need to become profitable first but will focus on culture next year.

Let's make one thing clear, there should not be a time that any business including more than two people declares that the culture is not a priority. This is a big mistake, one that can cause more harm to a company than leaders imagine.

Designing and clarifying the ideal culture for your business and your brand is like investing in an excellent navigation system. Without it, you'll likely get miserably lost and miss a lot of productivity and success opportunities. But with it, you know where your next stop is and the ideal ways to get there.

In any business, you cannot succeed without your people. Finding, engaging, sustaining, and maximising the right people in the right climate is the art and the science of culture.

#3 We don't have control over culture. It has to happen organically; it's in us.

I don't know how often I have heard stories about successful start-up owners whose business culture happens on its own and with excellent outcomes. Unfortunately, such captivating stories validate this somewhat misleading belief.

Especially in start-ups, in the early stages when there are fewer people, co-founders and early joiners form a small team. They have great times, work and party, and work harder. Success comes. And right after that, things begin to fall apart as they grow and grow. The founders become alienated from their own company as they find it moving away from their vision.

When culture is not designed, when the collective narrative is not the leaders' narrative, things get out of control very quickly. The power of one bad apple is more significant than you can imagine, hence the extreme importance of designing, actioning, and role-modelling the desired behaviour until it becomes strong.

There is so much more to think about, but for now, I'll close this chapter with one key conclusion. People are the most important assets of any business. As AI and ML take over, machines will replace humans more quickly than we hoped. But some human skills are not replaceable, such as emotional intelligence, creativity, critical decision-making, and intuition.

We need to revolutionise certain concepts and understand that like people, culture is a living and ever-evolving part of businesses and brands.

SO, WHAT'S NEXT?

I hope that we businesspeople begin to realise, after all those years of struggling for performance, of HR efforts, of lost opportunities to bring our brands to life, that culture was actually running the show. It can be scary to come to this realisation, due to the complex nature of culture and how difficult it is to tackle it. It takes time and effort, but more importantly, it takes **will and consistency**.

The true magic of brand-led culture comes to life when the key stakeholders of an organisation are united through strong leadership and listen to each other. Culture is not only a human resource matter, it's a leadership matter. People and brand need to create one team.

So, if you are going to take one action, I recommend that you create a core team and ask each other these questions:

- What is the ideal culture for our industry and our brand?
- On a scale of 1 to 10, how close do we think we are to that ideal culture scenario?
- What will we do to build a winning culture and how will we do it?
- What's stopping us?

These are powerful questions that are more easily asked than answered. But the answers might trigger a transformation for the better.

ABOUT THE AUTHOR:
NURCIN ERDOGAN LOFFLER

Partner

Nurcin is a devoted brand, marketing, and culture strategist with a background in psychology, strategy, and marketing to build sustained value through understanding the true needs of people.

She is obsessed with understanding human behaviour and building brands and brand-led cultures that will create unique experiences for both consumers and employees.

Nurcin has worked in four countries in Europe, Asia, and the Middle East and has held leading roles in business strategy, brand, and marketing in Fortune 500 companies, such as Logitech, DAN, Red Bull, BAT, and L'Oréal, leading teams and functions in more than 14 markets.

Through TOUGHLOVE, she has been supporting businesses, creating and building brands, and designing and developing cultures in which people and results will thrive.

Nurcin has a BA degree in Psychology from Bosporus University – Istanbul, and a master's degree in Marketing & Communications from Galatasaray University – Istanbul. She holds a certification from Harvard Business School in Disruptive Strategy.

She is also a certified Executive Coach, a yogi, and a mum.

See you in the Metaverse

ELENI KITRA

I love change. No matter how uncomfortable it seems to be, change gives me an extra push, a kick in the butt to think differently, be more open, and move forward.

Business transformation is an umbrella term for making radical changes in how businesses operate with the goal of improving operational, financial and cultural performance. It includes significant changes in personnel, processes, and technology. These transformations help your organisation compete, become more efficient, or make wholesale strategic pivots.

Business transformation and change management are intertwined; they are each about shifts. The aim is to make changes across all levels of an organisation to better align with its business strategy and division. Building for the future is an essential part of the transformation strategy. It requires a bold vision and an intentional execution plan that can combine the best segments of the physical and virtual worlds.

The future is 'by design', physical and virtual. It is co-habitational in a seamless and interoperable way. It has not been long since we all started talking about the Metaverse and how it can apply to our world today and in the future.

The Metaverse is inclusive of all virtual worlds, VR and AR, and many of its subfields. However, it is still challenging to define its applicability and measure the significant impact it will have on day-to-day business. We already have intelligent physical worlds like smart factories, autonomous vehicles, smart personal devices, intelligent cruise ships, and automated ports. Tomorrow we'll see these grow into smart communities, cities, and countries, where everything will mirror physical experiences.

Talking about smart cities, think of the place you live in, and then imagine how it could be more effective, offering enhanced citizen and government engagement, improved transportation, and safer communities, and providing new economic development opportunities. Dubai recently announced a new economic output metric, the Gross Metaverese Product, to measure the contribution of the Metaverse to its economy.

And purely digital worlds are expanding as well.

Major companies from all sectors (although all companies are now technology companies) are building in the Metaverse, offering their employees and partners major solutions to work and interact from anywhere. And a selection of very different brands – from art auction houses to car manufacturers, brewing companies, and luxury goods – have built creative marketing and advertising experiences in the Metaverse for their customers.

New consumer metaverses will transport us to almost any type of world we can imagine, to play games, socialise or relax. While technological barriers and a shortage of content have prevented mass adoption, virtual reality may become the next-generation platform for communication – displacing our need for physical travel and easing related energy consumption. New forms of immersive games, cinematic experiences, and news media will surely emerge that place audiences in the middle of events.

THE METAVERSE IS REAL, AND SO ARE YOU

Although we are in the early days of the Metaverse, businesses have tremendous opportunities. They can transform everything from how they interact with customers, to products and services offered, to production and distribution processes, organisational operations, and more. Many reports and studies show that two out of three global executives see the Metaverse as having a positive business impact on their organisations, with 42% believing that it will be a 'breakthrough' or 'transformational'.

Every year, more than $50B is spent on virtual goods. According to McKinsey, e-commerce in the Metaverse will comprise around $2 to $2.6 trillion. JP Morgan has found that the Metaverse will infiltrate every sector in the coming years, culminating in market opportunities worth more than $1 trillion in annual revenues.

SIMPLIFYING THE METAVERSE

Whatever we can do in the real world, we can do in this virtual world, from simple activities, such as talking to people and buying groceries, to more complex or sophisticated activities that demand multiple interactions. The latter might include meeting and working with people from around the world, celebrating a friend's birthday from another continent, or buying real estate and other assets in their digital form.

The internet is being reimagined, and enterprises need to be ready for what comes next across all aspects of Life and Business. One of the most critical areas is the new workplace; the Metaverse will be an absolute game changer for workspace and team collaboration.

The last 24 months have created many moments of truth for all of us as we've had to transition away from the office and constant physical interaction with colleagues and partners. Our lives used to be meeting after meeting, travelling around the world, delivering speeches and closing deals – just doing our job, without even thinking 'Is there any other way to do this?'.

And suddenly we had to turn all these habits upside down. We got 'video-call fatigue'.

Now we can bring everyone to the same room, overcoming any geographical limitations. VR Rooms will transform the workplace as we know it. In the Metaverse, people's ability to redefine the workspace according to their needs and deliverables is unprecedented. Opportunities range from brainstorming with your team and inspiring peers to generate ideas, to delivering training incorporating immersive experiences, to just hosting a team-building activity and making people feel comfortable.

We can create our own personas/avatars that can mirror ourselves in aspects such as voice and body language. Avatars are our digital representatives, like the characters we control in video games. And we will use them for all our interactions as we shop, socialise, learn and work in connected online environments. People can actually 'live' in the Metaverse through their digital personas and their avatars. And many companies are already using avatars for a number of operations, especially in the area of customer service, to handle multiple inquiries.

SHOPPING IN THE METAVERSE

Shopping in the Metaverse is changing how we buy things. A broad variety of companies, from furniture and home appliances to beauty and clothing, have been pioneering in the Metaverse, bringing to life immersive experiences that make shopping a second-nature activity. One of my favourite examples is what Gucci did for their 100th anniversary. They created a virtual art exhibition; customers entered as avatars and they could purchase virtual products that could be resold at a higher price.

Again, a user's avatar, the digital identity used to engage with other players in the virtual world, – is highly customisable. And yes! Companies need avatars, too; they will become their branding machines. Interaction between brands and their customers in this way will have a positive impact on engagement.

LEARNING EXPERIENCES

Education is changing dramatically across educational institutions, corporate training, and personal improvement. Nestle Purina, the global pet food industry leader, uses the Oculus for Business platform to drive efficiencies throughout its sales organisation. Training people in VR saves significant amounts in travel and lost productivity costs.

What speaks most to my heart is the unlimited opportunities the Metaverse is opening to the healthcare ecosystem, from VR counselling and telemedicine consultation (where patients can have access to an unlimited number of clinicians around the world) to surgeons using augmented reality technology to guide certain surgical procedures.

WHAT DOES THIS MEAN FOR BUSINESS?

The Metaverse presents new business opportunities, redefines the value chain, and levels up the customer lifecycle in a zero-friction mode. Even if your current audience is not yet familiar with this digital reality, your brand needs to build for it. By 2025, Gen-Z will account for one quarter of the global workforce. They feel very comfortable online and recognise little distinction between it and the physical world. Their attention span is relatively short, and it becomes shorter and shorter. According to several surveys, Gen Z's attention span is eight seconds, while Millennials' is 12 seconds. Every brand should build products and services for this generation. My Gen Z children remind me of this every single day.

Looking a bit more broadly, we need to recognise that we have a new type of customer, the Enhanced Customer, and we need to find a way to get closer to them. The enhanced consumer has clear expectations of what a brand should be able to offer and deliver to them. They are more knowledgeable than ever, as they have access to unlimited sources of information.

WE ARE IN THE ERA OF NOW

There are many things that companies can do to be Metaverse-ready. However, I understand that amid all this change, it is not easy to decide what works for your brand. So, I would like to introduce the FEED model, something that has helped me put things together in a simple yet clear way. FEED stands for Familiarise, Explore, Establish, and Determine.

1. **Familiarise** yourself. Read, get involved, and be open to learning from others. See the Metaverse through the eyes of your current and future customers.

2. **Explore** and experiment with new VR technologies and wearables and build on existing Metaverse platforms that can give you a good understanding of how things work. By doing so, you will be able to track the ongoing evolution amongst your teams and partners to restructure your business operation and redefine each stakeholder's role in your company.

3. **Establish** your innovation model, incremental or radical. Collaborate with existing Metaverse platforms that can help you bridge the gap between the physical and virtual worlds.

4. **Determine** the Metaverse's role in your business goals and develop use cases. See how relevant the Metaverse is to your business.

Be strategic about how you will leverage the Metaverse to connect with your consumers and empower them to best use your products and services and help you innovate your business. And be prepared to change as the Metaverse takes shape and you learn from it. During the last WEF (World Economic Forum 2022), the Metaverse was a key topic of discussion, especially in relation to how key industries will transform. Some of the most advanced industries to have incorporated the new technologies are Media & Entertainment, Sport, E-commerce, and Retail.

MEDIA & ENTERTAINMENT

Let's look closer at one of those industries. Unlimited creativity, unique immersive experiences, and new ecosystems – these are the three factors of success for the Media and Entertainment world. The goal of each is to enhance human interaction with brands and services in a parallel world. It is important to understand that Metaverse experiences are designed to be interconnected, to be felt as a part of a whole.

Well-known artists, like Imagine Dragons, Ariana Grande, Billie Eilish, Travis Scott, and numerous more have set up new music and entertainment journeys; it is more a kind of storytelling than just a one-off experience. According to PWC Global Entertainment and Media Outlook, Global entertainment and media revenues have surged to US$ 2.3 trillion. Virtual reality is seeing 36% growth, as gaming and esports are on pace to become a US$ 324 billion business. Players can go in and out of gaming platforms as they wish. They can also interact with other players, trade in numerous virtual assets, and spend and earn real money by selling their virtual assets via NFTs. They can have physical-like experiences through wearables such as glasses, gloves, and jackets.

The Metaverse is all about encouraging new avenues for human connectivity. Performances, tournaments, and other events that take place in the Metaverse (known as Massive Interactive Live Events, or MILEs) bring people together in real-time – if only virtually.

Singer The Weeknd used a digital avatar to perform on TikTok after the pandemic caused in-person concert cancellations. His virtual concert generated more than 2 million views. Gorillaz and Post Malone performed via an avatar in virtual venues, and Dua Lipa attended a runway show as her avatar. In April 2020, rapper Travis Scott drew in an audience of nearly 30 million viewers to his Fortnite MILE. Some artists even co-perform with their Metaverse avatars during real-world shows.

GAMING AND GAMIFICATION

I still remember when we launched Playstation almost 30 years ago. It was a fifth-generation game console, initiating a revolutionary era for the gaming industry and its target audience. Today gaming and gamification are redefining the customer experience and entertainment.

Gamification can create engaging customer experiences to improve how customers interact with a brand or firm; however, not all elements have the same effect on brand engagement. Gamification can apply in many areas such as Learning, Recruitment, Sales & Marketing, and Customer Service. It can increase brand awareness and brand loyalty. Working Metaverse games into your marketing strategy can encourage your target audience to interact directly with your brand and learn in detail what you offer and value.

E-COMMERCE AND RETAIL

We have already talked about shopping in the Metaverse. Here I would like to focus more on the true convergence that is brought between the physical and the virtual world. No brand can escape this massive transformation.

Simulating the real world in a virtual form is gaining popularity through the Metaverse. It offers consumers the opportunity to seamlessly walk through physical and virtual environments and purchase physical and virtual assets. In the last few years alone, NFTs have opened a multi-billion-dollar market that continues to grow daily. Yet, NFT technology is still very young.

NFTs are changing how we think about digital goods by allowing us to claim ownership and generate value by limiting supply. They have advanced the digital art market and laid the foundations for the Metaverse economy. Multiple brands offer users the option to claim their NFT. Recently a web3 social media platform called coto offered a limited number of NFTs to their community creators.

CUSTOMER VS. ENHANCED CUSTOMER, HOW TO GET CLOSER AND WIN THEM OVER

Here are four simple steps to consider. They can easily be applied to your Transformation Strategy. I have put them into the context of the FEED model.

1. **Familiarise** yourself with technology to get the best out of it. Nothing is too personal that you cannot do it now online, from trying new clothes to buying a new car, to experiencing a new place for vacation or having a personal session with your doctor. Leverage the current technologies such as AR & VR, and always be open to new platforms and features that will help you build an upgraded customer experience in a convergent physical and virtual world.

2. **Explore** how you can be where your customers are 24/7. Distance is not a problem anymore. The Customer Journey and Purchase Funnel have become shorter and better.

3. **Establish** an infinite number of touchpoints and digital assets. We need to think about how the Consumer Journey is pivoting from what people are experiencing in the current/physical world and leaping into a virtual, multi-dimensional, interconnected world.

4. **Determine** the way to go from Omnichannel to Hybrid to Metaverse. It is all about the interconnected world and how consumers are experiencing it. People do not set a line anymore between the physical and virtual worlds. They are experiencing this as a seamless ecosystem, where interactions happen without thinking about whether this is going to be a virtual or a physical engagement.

Lead the Future.

Harness the Technology.

Deliver the Impact.

ABOUT THE AUTHOR:
ELENI KITRA

Partner

Eleni has three decades of experience in Business Management, Digital Transformation, Communication and Marketing, leading international companies in multiple industries and geographies.

She has served as the Regional Head of Automotive and Mobility at Meta – ex Facebook – and she is a Partner of TOUGHLOVE Advisors, with a focus on Transformation Strategy and Mobility Ecosystems.

Eleni is a global leader in supporting women in Tech, and she is a passionate mentor and gender equality ambassador.

She is the Founder and CEO of PeopleFirst Group, an advisory firm helping companies to build diverse and inclusive organisations and achieve organisational excellence.

Eleni has been awarded multiple times for her work in digital and social media and she is a frequent speaker and presenter at regional and international conferences.

She is passionate about Youth and Academia and is Senior Lecturer for Digital marketing at Middlesex University.

The Power of a Human Truth

That One Insight that Changed the Game

MOHAMMED ISMAEEL HAMEEDALDIN

LET'S GO BACK IN TIME

Since this is a book about tough love, I feel it would be remiss of me not to start by telling you what tough love means to me. As with most things, it's probably best to start from the beginning, and for me that means going back 60 years or so to before I was born, to a time when everything changed for my family. 1962 marked the start of a 6-year revolution in Yemen, a revolution that led to the end of our family ruling the country, something we had done for centuries. This, to put it mildly, was a massive wake-up call for everyone. One moment you are ruling a country, the next you are in exile trying to establish a new life for yourself and your family. I was born in the last year of the revolution, and like most of my generation, I have only ever known the life I have today, one of studying hard, working hard and getting out of life what you put into it.

However, underpinning this new life was constant pressure from my parents, both to stay true to who we were as a family and to adapt to our new circumstances. Remember these are people, whose lives were turned upside down, who in the blink of an eye lost everything they had owned and loved.

It was more than just losing power and material things, it was about being forced to leave the only country, the only home, the only culture they had ever known. For some, the transition was harder than for others, but without exception, the generation that grew up in Yemen knew they had to prepare us for any eventuality. Having lost everything, they knew their role (like most parents I guess) was to ensure our future stability and success. Nothing was ever sugar-coated; there was a directness in their actions that was sometimes hard to accept. They knew they had to prepare us for a world where our family history wasn't going to save us (and at times could work against us), one where we needed to scramble and work hard to achieve what we wanted. This tough love wasn't always easy, but it became a foundation that I and most of my generation are grateful for, and one we have carried on with in our day-to-day engagements.

'THAT WON'T WORK HERE' SYNDROME

Now, let's look at a situation I'm sure many reading this will be able to relate to, the underlying tension often existing between corporate teams, be it local teams in the same function or teams across multiple markets. Have you ever heard any of these statements: 'that's not going to fly in our market', or 'that's not going to resonate with our consumers'? I know I have both said and heard them myself. There exists an innate desire to protect one's turf and a belief that other teams are just going to get in the way. If you are in a market, then you may see global teams as adding complexity and bureaucracy (and no value), so it's just easier and more efficient to do the work yourself. On the other hand, global teams can see markets as inefficient when they work alone, sometimes going off on tangents that don't reflect the global strategy, etc.

In this chapter we are going to explore the importance of truly investing your resources into understanding the needs of your audiences (both internal and especially external). When teams come together around their customers and define true insights or human truths, they can deliver greater efficiencies, more impactful work, and ultimately significant value to their overall bottom line. Whilst this chapter will look at all this through the lens of local and regional marketing teams working together, its learnings also apply to teams across different functions coming together more cohesively, be it in a single-market or multi-market scenario.

If you have ever been part of a diverse multi-functional or multi-market team, at some point you have experienced a time when its members had to put aside their local needs and focus instead on the greater good for the company. This will seem counterintuitive to some, as it may impact local objectives or even impact their business targets (at least in the short term). This was exactly the situation I found myself in as I joined Visa to lead the Marketing function for the CEMEA region (Central and Eastern Europe, Middle East and Africa). I had already been in a regional leadership role before this, whilst at HSBC, but that involved 17 similar markets in the same region (the Middle East and North Africa), with a consistent language and very similar cultures. In my new role

I was responsible for five teams across four sub-regions that comprised 90 very diverse countries, from Russia to South Africa. To make matters even more complicated, I had never worked in Eastern European markets before, so this was a totally new culture for me. CEMEA was a newly formed region, and I was one of 14 or so functional leaders – all of whom were external hires, and so all new to Visa and its ways of working. Basically, we were the new kids on the block, all of us having the same objective of establishing a new region, as opposed to a cluster of disconnected markets working in isolation. Some teams were receptive to what I and others aimed to do, but there was still the old guard to deal with. They had entrenched habits and a very strong 'this is how we do things here' mentality; this led to resistance to any change we wished to implement.

SHOW ME THE MONEY!

To help you understand where this resistance came from, I'll explain what the situation was like when we joined. First, it's important to say that nothing was broken; the markets were doing extremely well. Financially, the business was run at a local/sub-regional level. They owned the P&L and were responsible for the day-to-day business decisions. So why was there a need for change at all? I have worked in global organisations that were highly centralised, and others where decision-making was much more dispersed. Both models have pros and cons, and companies tend to switch between the two over time anyway. With local empowerment, market leaders feel they are more focused on their direct needs; there are fewer distractions from 'external parties'; they feel more in control of their business, and ultimately feel they can make decisions faster as they aren't jumping through many layered hoops of approvals. These are all valid points; however, when each market looks at its P&L in isolation from the wider organisation, it is very difficult for the larger corporate entity to drive efficiencies from its global scale. It's not an either/or decision here. It's about finding the happy medium where the changes make sense to everyone (well at least as many people as possible). I was specifically looking at this through the lens of my Marketing team, which is often where the largest 'discretionary' budgets sit – and potentially where significant efficiencies could be found. The principles here could apply equally across any function, but I will focus on the specifics of what I did in Marketing

With any change, it is important to identify who controls the purse strings if you want to get any real traction. We were a very matrixed organisation. Each of the four sub-regions was managed by a General Manager who owned its P&L and was responsible for the sale targets (and the sales teams). Whilst the functions were managed centrally, (i.e., Marketing reported to me in the hub), their primary role was in support of their regional GM and his or her business objectives. The worst thing for my team, and for the business itself, would have been to expect my team to choose between me and the GM. A united front was key. I was fortunate enough to work with exceptional business leaders who could see the bigger picture, especially when the value to their markets was highlighted to them. However, they couldn't be involved in the day-to-day goings on of every activity. Often, they just didn't see the value, or they weren't made aware of opportunities and therefore didn't see any incentive to look at other options. Basically, things were working well for them, so why should they disrupt their teams? Good business leaders are usually very pragmatic. So I focused on showing them what I intended to achieve and what it would mean for them and their business. This made it much easier to get their buy-in to the planned changes.

As a marketer myself for over 25 years now, I can tell you that if you give individual marketers a budget, nine times out of ten they are going to want to spend it on creating work for their own markets. They are unlikely to voluntarily search out colleagues in other markets to work on a mutually beneficial project. It's not always clear why they need to do things differently and basically what's in it for them. Instead, they see possible drawbacks. They might lose creative control or have to share the limelight with someone else. The work itself might be diluted across so many different markets and audiences, which could lead to less impactful work.

It was clear that if I were to make any dents into the way my new team worked, then I was going to have to invest sufficient time in showcasing to them the value they would get – personally, professionally, and to their bottom line – from working in a more connected way with their colleagues from across the region. It was also important to reassure them that not everything was changing; there would still be a level of autonomy at the local level, and we were only looking to focus on the key strategic pillars that were consistent across markets.

FINE, BUT WHAT'S IN IT FOR ME?

To this point I had worked for organisations that employed anywhere between 250,000 and 300,000 people. Now I found myself working for the fifth most powerful brand in the world, but at the time the global business was being run by just 9,500 employees. I would need to find a different way of working if I were to deliver the results I'd set myself. I no longer had a huge network to fall back on, in fact, there were just 50 marketers in my team responsible for all 90 countries. This group was made up of small teams in the bigger markets, but we also had sole contributors scattered across the region responsible for the smaller countries. Many of them had no real sense of a team, the geographical distance keeping them from interacting with their colleagues. Whilst they needed support, they often didn't know how to ask for it – even if they could ask in the first place. What was clear, however, was that they all wanted to be part of something bigger.

And whilst building a more connected team was a key objective for me, the glaring opportunity I saw as soon as I arrived was to reduce costs. I joined Visa in the middle of the annual planning cycle in 2014 and my onboarding was literally the next fiscal year's plans. The four sub-regions of the CEMEA region built their plans locally (i.e., at a P&L level). I saw it as a fantastic way to entrench myself into the new business; the individual plans themselves were incredibly thorough and well designed. However, once I'd had the opportunity to review all four plans, it became clear that they were very similar, with consistent strategies simply dialled up or down as relevant to that specific region. There was nothing wrong with having the same priorities, but each region was going about delivering those priorities separately. For the head of a sub-region, working against specific market needs makes obvious sense. It's not until you ladder up the four plans to the full CEMEA level that you start to see the inefficiencies. Four sub-regions working separately on the same marketing strategies meant that we were paying our agencies four times to help us solve a single regional need.

It was obvious we had an opportunity to work differently, to connect up as one regional team instead of four teams spread across 90 markets. But for this to happen we needed to plan very differently and start the whole planning process much earlier so that we gave ourselves enough time to align properly. This was where the idea of a Hub team, to sit across the four regions, comes into play. It was a neutral team to support all regions equally, one that took a holistic view of the full region to bring all parties together to work more cohesively. For this to happen, we needed to double down on showing them what was in it for the sub-regions, especially the larger, 'richer' ones who felt there was no value for them in changing how they worked – after all, they already had the resources they needed; this was someone else's problem to fix, not theirs.

We focused on four key areas that would apply to all regions, no matter how large or small they were: budgets, resources, access to quality work and people development.

1. Focusing on a single brief on behalf of the whole region would allow the teams to pool their funds together against

a consistent strategy and in so doing reduce costs for the individual markets whilst still delivering on their respective needs. This would create incremental savings that could be allocated against additional plans.

2. This would also allow the markets to pool their resources more effectively, so they wouldn't have multiple people in every market duplicating work. This not only helped create capacity, something crucial in a small regional team; by incorporating people from different markets they were also getting very diversified perspectives going into the work itself, making it more well-rounded.

3. Having these pooled resources working on a brief for multiple regions (versus just a single market or sub-region) they were getting exposure to new skills. Project management occurred on a much wider scale than was previously possible. They had exposure to markets and culture previously beyond their reach – and now with the scale of the projects much larger, they were also receiving exposure to senior regional management beyond their markets.

4. And lastly, smaller markets have access to smaller budgets, so producing all that they want and to a high standard is often not possible. Whilst they could take off the shelf solutions from other markets, they weren't always fully fit for purpose; however, with this new model they were part of the consideration set from the design phase, making the work more impactful for them.

IT'S NOT ALWAYS SMOOTH SAILING – AND THAT'S OK

Now, I'd love to say that it was all smooth sailing from there, but not everyone bought into the proposed changes, with some teams being more vocal about it than others. Unsurprisingly, it was the largest markets that felt they were getting the short end of the stick with these changes. Markets like Russia and the UAE felt they did not have enough in common with markets like Nigeria or Egypt, for example, to justify the upheaval (as they saw it) of coming together as one team. So, we agreed not to take the full plunge from the start, but to pilot one initiative and see how things went from there. One should never assume you have buy-in until you see it first-hand. We agreed that each sub-region would own a strategy on behalf of CEMEA as a whole and the respective strategies would be led by the region with the most affinity and need for it in terms of their business. So, for example, Russia would lead the work on Premium Cards, MENA would lead Cross-Border business (travel), and Sub-Saharan Africa on Everyday Spends (spends on small everyday purchases, not just the big monthly shop). What this meant in practice was that one region would be the overall lead; however, all regions had a voice throughout the development process. The initial brief was worked on by all regions, ensuring their top-level needs were built in; then it was handed over to the lead market to take forward with our agency partners. The regions were also pulled in at specific checkpoints to ensure they could provide feedback before the work was finalised.

This meant that everyone had skin in the game, that the work reflected the business needs of the regions, and that what was produced would be relevant to the market dynamics (demographics, stage of market development, etc). Ensuring that all regions had a voice in the process also drove accountability: they couldn't pass the buck later, decide to produce their own work and blame the lead market.

AND THEN IT ALL MADE SENSE

The first pilot we ran was on the Everyday Spends strategy led by the team in Africa. All the regions worked on the brief, ensuring they fed in insights from their markets. Unfortunately, the first draft was extremely weak. The input from the regions was little more than 'google-insights' as I call them, general observations that were virtually useless. Clearly, some markets were still having issues releasing the reins to another region to develop work on their behalf. We needed to regroup and ensure that the input into the brief would do it justice. Therefore, we created a consistent questionnaire for each member of the working group from across the four regions, who were required to personally conduct direct-to-consumer interviews and report back on what they found. And it's what the teams came back with that was truly the gamechanger. When forced to really invest in understanding their consumers and delve into their daily lives, every one of the regions came back with the exact same human truth. *It was at this moment that everything changed, and it was the power of a great insight that made all the difference!*

This was the moment everyone stopped focusing on differences and could finally see the possibilities.

So, what was that insight? Well, it was very simple, but something that every one of the team could relate to at a very personal level:

Mothers all over, be it in Russia or Nigeria, get up with the same human drive – they battle every day to give the very best they can for their families and scramble to find even the smallest ways to make their lives and that of their family's that little bit better. Whether she has to walk five miles every day to sell her goods in the market or commutes to work in a high-rise building, she gets up and works hard to find value in her daily life. For this target audience, big offers, chances to win glamorous holidays, etc. are just too distant and unlikely to happen. They are looking for consistent tangible benefits, where they can see value every day and with every purchase.

From this insight the first pan-regional campaign (known as #SmallWins) was born across the CEMEA region. And whilst the work originated from one insight, it manifested itself in different ways across the region; markets could tailor the work to their needs whilst remaining consistent with the core idea. The real test of this new way of working was in the results. In addition to seeing a 25% reduction in our total agency fees over the next fiscal year, we saw a significant increase in the number of markets adopting the work produced 'centrally' by each of the regions. Perhaps the most impactful result was on the team itself, which became one of the most connected teams across the whole of CEMEA. Collaboration became second nature to them. Working as one large team led to the highest engagement scores of any marketing team at Visa.

One would have had every right to think that a change of this scale could not succeed, especially considering the range of markets, nationalities, languages and religions that make up CEMEA. However, when you put differences aside and focus on the bigger picture, magic can truly happen. And this is how the power of the humble insight changed the way we did business.

AND IT'S A WRAP!

I've presented this chapter through the lens of marketing, but the principles here could apply to any group of people or combination of teams. CEMEA is not a geographic region; if you think about it, it feels like one thrown together for no other reason than these countries didn't fit nicely anywhere else. The diversity is perhaps as wide as you'll see anywhere, so if you ever find yourself thinking the differences you are facing are too extreme to bridge or that your needs are unique, then take a second to think about how 90 countries, five separate teams, and 50 individual team members could come together and solve issues as one team. Then think about what's truly stopping you.

So, before I wrap things up, I wanted to leave you with some thoughts that have helped me as I've tried to navigate my journey:

- Progress will only happen if you are comfortable with change, so if something doesn't feel right to you, or you think it can be done better, then ask yourself, what's stopping you? Always be ready to challenge the status quo, because you never know what lies on the other side of change. Any time I hear the words 'this is how we do things here' I know that's where my attention should go first, if for no other reason than this is probably an area of the business that just hasn't been looked at for a while.
- Always start by identifying the key decision makers, those who are either going to be obstacles along the way or those who will facilitate your journey. Try to understand their needs and concerns early on.
- Always remember that you are most likely working with passionate people, so be clear with them about the issues you are hoping to address, how you will go about it, and most importantly, what it will ultimately deliver for them. Just like you, they have goals to deliver every year – as much as possible, let the numbers do the talking for you. Whether it's lower costs, incremental revenue or simply better efficiencies, few will turn away the opportunity to perform better.
- Be ready for failure and be comfortable with the fact that sometimes things won't go as planned. More importantly, be ready to get right back up again and not let these

setbacks distract you from the ultimate objective. Learn from them and move on.

- Finally, and most importantly, never cut corners when it comes to understanding your audience, whether your end customers or your internal audience whose help you need to bring things to life. Understand what is truly important to them and dig till you find that human truth that helps you unlock a barrier or opportunity in someone's mind

ABOUT THE AUTHOR:
MOHAMMED ISMAEEL HAMEEDALDIN

Partner

Mohammed brings 30 years of experience across varied multi-national blue-chip firms. Starting his career in finance, his real passion is in the field of Marketing, where he has spent the last 25 years in diverse marketing functions, including Insights, Marketing Strategy, Planning and Consulting, Sponsorship & Events, Product & Brand Marketing as well as all aspects of Social, Digital and Data-led Marketing.

He's a strong believer in marketing as a business function, with a real focus on the value it brings to the bottom line.

Starting his career at Citibank, he spent the next 10 years at P&G, followed by a similar stint at HSBC before finally moving to Visa Inc, where he spent the last seven-plus years as the SVP of Marketing across 90 Markets.

Mohammed was the executive sponsor for both the Mental Health and Wellness and the Women's Leadership Networks at Visa. Both are areas he is extremely passionate about and areas he continues to champion to this day.

Making Right Turns

EDDIE MAALOUF

Spending decades looking back at whether you should have made a right or left turn is not healthy. However, making the best from each turn you take will probably pay you back.

Looking back at life post high school (1986), I can't help but think of the choices I made and the impact they have had. I also cannot help but assess what my life would have looked like had I made a left turn instead of a right. This is not a feeling of remorse but rather a sense of venture and curiosity, a characteristic trait that others seem to have noticed about me (as well as my constant 'unintended' frown).

My venturer character emanates from my childhood wandering across continents. Raised in West Africa and high schooled in Lebanon during the civil war, I had two passions in life, football and photography. I decided to pursue both of them, hoping to make career of at least one. Needless to say, neither worked out as planned. My attempt at co-authoring this book was also not a plan. Talk about turning points.

I was a university drop-out, unknown to my parents…shhhhhh! I just wanted to play football. So, with hardly an associate degree from my university in Spain in 1988, I started my professional life in 1990 when I travelled to Paris hoping to get a job. Which

I did – it was a very basic, low-paying merchandising job for which I was grateful. I am more grateful that this job introduced me to someone who decided to take a chance on me by offering me a job in advertising in Dubai. That was my first right turn. 1992! That was also the start of my career in marketing.

DRIVE WITH PASSION NOT REVENGE.

As marketers, we rarely understand the role and its expectations. This is not only driven by our own obliviousness but is mostly a product of weak or inaccurate job expectations from organisations that don't necessarily understand what is expected from marketing. Bottom line: we tend to become victims of our anticipations.

In hindsight, it feels like I spent the first two decades of my career challenging the status quo of every role and every challenge I had faced. It must be the curious venturer in me that drove me to constantly question what was being done and why. In 2008, I set up my own company, driven by some sense of convoluted revenge against the challenges I had faced. I quickly realised that all the questioning and dubiousness I carried was taking a toll on me, on my self-confidence and my life balance; nothing was sufficient, professionally speaking. That was when I decided to adopt the simple, straight forward, and candid approach to making business work. I guess by then I had realised that all the tough love I had received and given myself had started to create some effect. That was my second right turn; 2012, when I exited my company unplanned and unfulfilled.

Keep this in mind: do not succumb to what you are told your role is, but rather keep your focus on what it should be. You will be surprised by how deviating from what people believe a role to be – to what you can actually deliver from that role – becomes nothing less than the welcome change of success!

Typical leading questions around what you bring to the table are almost always the perfect segue to what the role should actually bring to an organisation. Usually, the onboarding process revolves around salaries, titles, bonuses, team structures, etc. When was the last time any of us asked, 'what does success look like?', 'what tools, teams, insights, and portfolios are at our disposal to achieve such success?', and 'what is my role in getting the organisation there?'

This is not the result of our lack of focus or knowledge but is rather driven by a pre-construed notion of what we were told the job needed, as opposed to what it *actually* needs. This misconception can lead to failure.

WHAT'S ON THE TABLE?

I wish there were a pre-determined set of deliverables and expectations for the marketing role common to all organisations, agendas and leadership teams. There aren't any.

I have since realised that managing 'the agenda' as opposed to the role is the correct right turn to make. 'What do you bring to the table?' is a question too commonly asked. I find it a bit pretentious and usually return the favour by asking "what's on the table?" Understanding the challenge is not the same as understanding the role and the difference can be catastrophic sometimes. It has been for me on multiple occasions.

My 'Right Turn 2012' was a simplification approach I adopted to address all my future challenges. Do not mistake a 'simple approach' with the process or the need to find a solution. Both might yield complex processes to arrive at a solution. Also remember that identifying the pain point is half the battle; this is the process that should be made simple. Finding a solution to that pain point may require a complex approach, but with a clear target in mind the complexity becomes manageable.

Let's answer the question I raised earlier, 'What do you bring to the table?'.

HOW DO WE KEEP IT SIMPLE.

You are a creator of demand. This means you will do whatever it takes with whatever is needed to build growth – whatever growth means: volume, value, awareness, retention, etc. – as long as it is aligned with the organisation's definition of growth.

Now that we understand where the misconceptions lie, let me share my personal experience after decades of mastering the role by making many mistakes on the way. Today, I clarify three simple but crucial facts before accepting any challenge.

1. Define the organisation's pain point or points. There might be more than one and they might be contradictory. I have seen organisations suffer from margin erosion while sales increased and others who defined their growth in value and not volume.

2. Try to understand what the definition of success is and draw the finish line. Nobody expects us to get them to that line in one move.

3. Now that you know the challenge (pain point) and have a better understanding of the expectations (success defined), it's important to get a feel about how committed the organisation is to achieve this success. Understanding the level of competencies, people, tools, and budgets available becomes the acid test. Not having these support platforms is not the problem, not wanting to have them is. This what you need to confirm before accepting the challenge.

Having such clarity at the outset allows us to decipher the needs from the haves. It also makes it easier to gauge the chances of success and gives us some comfort in terms of addressing the challenge and being successful.

Pain points are usually opportunities. Losing market share means the opportunity to gain it exists.

For businesses, the formula for success is getting the right mix between sizing the opportunity, the organisational means to address that opportunity, and the alignment of what success means across the organisation through clear objectives and key results (OKRs) settings – all of which is set against a timeline.

SPELL IT OUT PLEASE!

Think of the following relationship formula:

GROWTH = Opportunity Size x Organisational Capability / Time

Sounds easy. Yet we all know it's never that simple. Our role is to keep it simple by analysing the data and the givens against this formula.

Here's some perspective based on my years in telecom. I was once handed over a volume growth mandate of 23%, year on year, for a market where my market share was over 65% and the market's annual growth rate was 16%!

All things being equal, I could have achieved 65% of the 16% market growth opportunity (10.4%), which is a far cry from the 23% growth target. In simple math, I needed to capture the entire market growth (16%) while gaining an incremental 7% from competitors! Not a task I would accept lightly.

I started looking at new growth areas to bridge the 13% gap (23% – 10.4%) I needed to get to my target. Purchase trends showed that 34% of the addressable buyer population was unaddressed because they fell short on the ability to afford a mobile phone. There was a potential growth market of 34% in volume if I could introduce a low-end handset (sub $63) to expand mobile user penetration. This meant a port-folio expansion, a new production line launch, a change in procurement strategy … etc. It also meant a change in the distribution channel, catering to the new buyer's market, and other go-to-market alterations.

When presented to the leadership team, the plan failed at the cost of a new production line – until we realised that this new 'sub $63' product line meant entry to over 28 other emerging markets that were previously untapped due to the similar lack of affordability within the portfolio.

Plug these givens into the growth formula:

GROWTH @ 23% = 16% + 34% Opportunity Size x 0% Organisational Capability / 1 year

Organisational capability was set at 0%, since the production line needed eight months to be ready; hence the 23% ended at the initial organic growth of 10% in year one. However, for year two, this proved extremely successful with new markets opening up.

As marketers, our role is to create a demand wave that drives business, whether by building brands, expanding markets and categories or developing portfolios and channels. Our ability to think laterally is what makes us successful. Becoming the person (or team) that everyone seeks for solutions – that's when you know you are doing something right!

You may ask, how did this growth insight come into play?

Remember how 2012's right turn meant keeping it simple? In this example the answer to the three questions were:

1. The pain point is lack of growth opportunity with the current portfolio in the current markets. The math did not add up.
2. Success was defined by the ability to venture into new consumer segments, which meant new portfolio introductions (affordable handsets) and new markets where the concentration of these consumer segments was big enough to warrant the investment
3. Looking at the organisation's risk appetite, it was clear that the interest was high; extremely high because the returns were even higher. It meant production facilities, new market entries and more support on the ground.

Let's talk process. Having analysed my experiences (the successful ones and those that taught me) I have realised that the process is quite simple, so simple that I wish I had had that structure in my early days. I am now hoping you can benefit from this thinking process.

STRUCTURING YOUR THOUGHTS WHEN APPLYING.

Let me cement this simple approach to the extent that you can now take it and use it with pride. I'm sure we can agree that the path to growth is all about progress and that progress is manifested in many ways, shapes and forms.

Defining our roles becomes congruent with *three* key pillars that together form the essence of all business marketing operations, regardless of the industry or the market or the product/service you represent. These pillars build what I will call the 'Marketing Operations Eco-system'. This chapter is my attempt to explain these pillars and the interaction among them to optimise the outcome of progress – to achieve growth.

What are the three pillars?

- Market Opportunity & Analytics → Understanding where to sell, what, for how much and to whom. Sizing the opportunity.
- Competencies, Tools & Capabilities → Ensuring that the right people, the right competencies and the right tools can deliver against the business opportunity.
- Business Objectives → Defining success metrics based on the business needs and the ability to track them (**OKRs**).

Operational tasks, no matter what they may be, will fall under one of these *three* pillars. Let's take a deep dive to understand what these pillars are and how they interact with one another.

1. Market Opportunity & Analytics

These are what bring a business into existence in the first place. If there is a demand in a market then there is an opportunity to fulfil that demand, hence venturing into that market becomes a viable business opportunity.

MADE WITH TOUGHLOVE

That's good to know, but it's not enough!

It is also necessary to run gap analyses to size and locate the exact opportunity, the profile of consumers and the channels where these opportunities navigate. Price is important and so is the format of the product (packaging, product variants, competition, etc.).

This pillar is our starting point. Everything is decided based on the findings and insights gained from investigating a market opportunity. Understanding the dynamics behind the market is important to serving that demand competitively.

Once the opportunity has been defined, mapping your portfolio against it is also crucial. Do I have the right product with the right characteristics to compete for a share of that segment? What do I need to become market ready? Based on the physical attributes of the product-to-product support and product pricing, do I have the capability to reach and distribute? And the list goes on.

Ask yourself this: who is responsible for mapping the 'Market Opportunity' and how is it done?

2. Competencies, Tools & Capabilities

Having the right people with the right competencies and tools, and experience to pursue such opportunities is your second pillar. This is not only the role responsibility of

106

Human Resources. Remember, HR doesn't necessarily know what they need until we tell them what we need. People's competencies will extend from marketing and beyond. While the 'beyond' is not for us marketers to determine, it remains an output of our Market Opportunity definition (gap analysis), which has identified roles needed to compete successfully in our go-to market. Consumer needs spring from portfolio development. Pricing, market entry strategy, channel development, supply chain and route to market, sales and consumer demand generation and fulfillment are all part of the same ecosystem needed to deliver on growth against the identified market opportunity.

You've probably started seeing the importance of Pillar 1 in relation to Pillar 2. Marketing is now at the intersection of Market opportunities and People and Organisational capabilities; although they might not be solely responsible for both, they surely are in the driver's seat.

Now ask yourself this. How do these pillars interact?

3. The Business Objectives

While this one seems obvious, we should avoid taking it for granted. Alignment across all organisational verticals on clear objectives is imperative to achieving growth. Undersupply is as devastating as oversupply. Wrong pricing means pricing yourself out of the market or leaving money on the table. Wrong positioning of products or services also means missing the target and the opportunity.

This pillar is usually driven by the leadership team. We might also start from a business objective and work backwards towards Pillars 1 and 2. They are by no means sequential, yet they should coexist: this is not an either-or scenario.

These objectives are usually aligned with many milestones across multiple deliverables and stakeholders. They are not only financial or sales milestones, and they should take into account *all* streams independently to ensure that the entire ecosystem is quantified and that deliverables are clear across the plan and at every point of engagement with the right stakeholder accountability.

BUILD THAT RELATIONSHIP.

This takes me to the relation that exists between these pillars. The simplest way to explain this is by saying 'spot the opportunity in the market that drives demand'. Ensure there is a product in the portfolio that delivers. Recruit the team that is needed to deliver it. Define and quantify the success factors and objectives. The more cohesive the team is to the market opportunity and the more aligned the objectives are to the team and the opportunity, the greater the progress will be and the bigger the growth. It is that simple.

The formula becomes obvious as you visualise the overlap of people's capabilities, market opportunity, and a business objective that quantifies this opportunity. The more they overlap the greater the growth potential expands!

So, by continuously optimising the alignment between these pillars – through better planning of the market opportunity with the people responsible and setting the right objectives – you will tend to achieve higher growth!

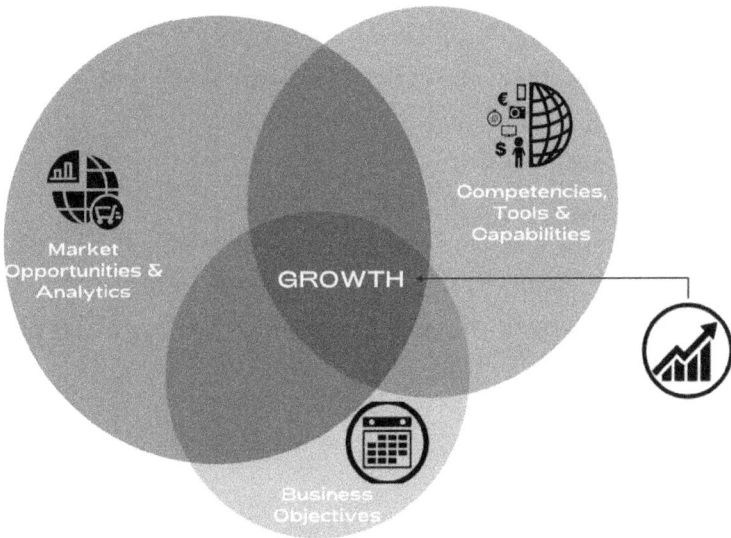

At ToughLove we have made it our mission to help organisations and leaders focus on these pillars. We help them to understand the level of integration and alignment across independent teams in the organisation and their leadership team, for each of these pillars and in relation to set objectives.

Now that the principle has been simplified, let's look at what it means to us as accountable professionals and responsible leaders – not only to understand the ask but also to be able to plan it and deliver on it.

Exploring roadblocks is the best place to start. It allows us to plan for success and helps prevents loss of interest along the way (better known as a lack of motivation). I always like to start at the top. Understanding what the leadership team wants, and being inquisitive about what they need, allows me to plant seeds about what I need to do to deliver on these pillars. Here are some questions I usually ask; they should help you formulate your own.

- What is the size of market X for product Y?
- How is it split between us and our competitors?
- What has been the movement of growth over the past X years?
- Where do we stand? Why?
- Who is the consumer base buying into these products and why?

Always make sure the source of any answers given to such questions is reliable. (Are they based on estimates or market data?) They will allow you to get a sense of how big the opportunity gap is. Growth potential or addressable market, as I like to call it.

Remember that this is a scientific process based on research and not a guessing game. (Many pretend to know the markets and use their internal sales and distribution data to quantify the gap opportunity.) Gathering research-based data shows that an organisation spares no effort to understand the market and the portfolio and that they are willing to invest in knowledge that leads to growth. This is the best outcome one could wish for.

Some organisations might lack such data. While this might sound catastrophic, it can sometimes be a blessing in disguise. Organisations that have gone to market on an opportunity hunch often don't pause to revisit these markets and better understand them. Think of face mask businesses during the initial days of the pandemic. The struggle was about supply, with no focus on market size and product definition – at least until the market became flooded and some traders lost what they had earned, and then some.

Organisations might be willing to embrace change and invest in knowledge, but not if we are incapable of presenting the outcome (value) in doing so. I say it's up to us to reshape these organisations and guide them through the three pillars by managing expectations on outcomes over a sensible timeline and showing the value in sustainable results. Such scenarios need not be negatively absorbed; they can be an opportunity to create massive change for growth within such companies. Crawl, walk and then run – that's the best way forward.

I introduced cost of market data as part of a marketing budget, many organisations do that. Here's a tip: I like to operate with buckets of budgets where permitted:

1. Working Marketing budget – this bucket carries all investments into marketing that work directly for the portfolio. Media, content, POS, sponsorships and the likes.
2. Non-Working Marketing budget – this bucket is where I tuck some money for indirect costs that are crucial for the optimisation of the Working Marketing Budget. The likes of agency retainers, research cost, people cost and other indirect but important-to-have costs.

This budgeting format also allows for better assessment of ROI simply calculated against Working Budgets. This is a conversation for another day, but it gives you a way to bypass the negative answer of 'we don't have the budget for research.'

Let's get back to our main discussion. Delving into details of each pillar is important to better plan the process, identify stakeholders who will be impacted, and pinpoint potential outcomes.

1. Market Opportunity & Analytics:

   This pillar is responsible for answering and addressing the following data points:

   • The market size in volume and value
   • The market location by channel
   • The price range of the market and its segments
   • The buyers of these products

- The purchase drivers or prohibitors
- The key competitors and how we compare to them
- The current state of what we have to address these gaps (portfolio and brand)
- The missing elements to Go-To-Market (channel coverage, manufacturing capacity, brand, price competitiveness … etc.)

Combining the answers to the above insights and data knowledge allows us to 'Qualify Gaps'. This means identifying a business opportunity in a market that we can address with minimal hindrance. Because the output might yield multiple gaps, and each might have a different level of readiness, a prioritisation plan will be needed. This plan starts with the low-hanging opportunities and moves to the least-ready gap in the market.

The output of such an exercise should deliver a GTM (Go to Market) plan that addresses the following:

- Portfolio definition of products
- Pricing strategy
- Channel & sales strategy
- Brand marketing strategy with defined consumer audience
- Manufacturing roadmap (including procurement planning)
- Financial plans (financial viability to address the 'gap')
- Business objectives towards the 'opportunity gap'

2. Competencies, Tools & Capabilities:

The success of such plans relies heavily on people's competencies and organisational capabilities to deliver on each of these sub-plans. This second pillar starts with co-creating sub-plans with each stakeholder. Stakeholders are accountable teams in their respective areas of expertise:

- Portfolio definition – typically driven by the head of operations in each organisation. He/she must be briefed on the opportunity gap and start designing/amending products to deliver to that identified market gap. Portfolio definition also requires the assurance that the right portfolio team is in place to deliver such products at the right price, quality level, and time.
- Channel and sales planning – driven by business development and sales. This plan means a simple integration of a 'new' product into an existing or new channel. Route to Market is a key component to success. Getting products on the right shelves using the most efficient route is crucial. Of course, supply chain management needs to be involved in this process. An output of a forecasted sales plan becomes the key deliverable.
- Manufacturing planning – ensuring that sourcing/manufacturing can cater to the forecasted demand and that procurement is aware of the need to deliver such a product with the right quantity and quality and at the right frequency.

- Brand marketing – It goes without saying that this is an extremely important factor to drive demand generation and awareness about a new offering to the right audience. See the other chapters that address brand building for more insights.
- Financial planning – the last stop on the train to launch. A good opportunity spotted doesn't always mean a good business decision. Financial planning needs to qualify the offering from manufacturing to on-shelf presence and promotion. The entire value-chain disruption necessary to meet this gap opportunity needs to be financially viable (without compromise) to ensure success. Opening new channels might mean massive investments. So will equipping factories with new machinery or even opening markets from scratch. Ensuring financial viability allows us to ascertain financially healthy propositions before embarking on them.

One more thing should be added, and that is the crucial dynamic of having the right competencies in place to deliver such a seamless plan. We now have an opportunity that has been vetted and planned and is ready to be driven by a team of competent experts.

3. Business Objectives:

There are many ways to tackle this simple task, but it can be a very delicate matter. It sets an expectation, a definition for success, and it comes with a lot of account-ability across the organisation.

Setting objectives means looking at all the sub-plans and ensuring they are in sync, in terms of deliverables and timelines.

The easiest way to explain the importance of getting this right is as follows. Exercise your math skills. If you set a market share objective of 10% for a market gap opportunity sized at 1 million SKUs/year while your manufacturing capacity in the year is restricted to ONLY 600,000 SKUs, then you are planning for failure.

The best way to set these objectives is to start north of the value chain and work your way to consumer take-off! Better yet, map these objectives in alignment with your ramp-up plans over multiple years to include the dynamics of seasonality, brand marketing and channel coverage against key milestones.

Another visual representation of the process will help walk you through the logic. (Remember to retain the freedom to customise this process based on your needs, industry or the type of product you are selling.)

As marketers in this era, our roles can vary greatly. They depend on many factors, ranging from our confidence in driving such a business operational planning model to leadership's appetite for allowing such levels of change to be driven by marketing.

YOUR ROLE DRIVEN BY PRINCIPLES.

I realise this does not answer an important question, namely, 'so what is my role in all of this?'.

I will share how I have tackled this issue in the past. I usually set some principles that I believe were a must for success in my previous roles in marketing. Here are some of them:

- No taking on responsibilities for tasks and objectives that I could not at least influence from an outcome perspective.
- Subjectivity in business is not welcome.

- Working in silos is not for me. 'You worry about your marketing plans, and we will worry about sales planning' never works.
- Portfolio management should be at the core of my responsibility.
- Pricing dynamics should always require my input. Pricing at the bottom of the price pyramid while positioning as a luxury product doesn't work.
- Lack of visibility on financial health is not an option. I need to understand the health indicators for the business to make some decisions (budgetary, expansion, diversification, etc.).
- Operating without a clear plan, a defined budget and aligned expectations should be forbidden.

These principles could require temporary compromises at times. At others, they challenged me to lift the role of marketing to include what I believe is a crucial component, and that is business marketing operations.

Today, I thrive on the capability to bring operational perspective into the marketing realm. Not only does it make our role more prominent and allow us to better deliver, but it also bridges a century-old divide between business operations and marketing. Let me explain what I mean. Professionally, I was raised to believe that sales and marketing never align. It took me some lashing to figure one thing out: the myth that marketers spend what sales make is only true if marketers allow it to be!

I fell victim to the divide and wasted some years struggling in the shadows to make a difference. Then I realised that the solution lies in changing from a passive-support, brand-only role to a business-insight, consumer-based role.

DATA NEVER LIES.

My parting wisdom in this chapter is this: start talking *Revenue* and stop talking only about *Brands*. While we all know that great brands yield greater revenues, the battle to convince leadership teams sometimes becomes exhausting. Speaking their language of revenue is a bridging strategy that almost instantaneously opens doors to everything we want to do as marketers, which should never exclude revenue generation.

As of today, stop what you are doing on brands and start looking at markets and consumers. Figure out why strong brands and campaigns sometimes fail to sell. The answer is always simple if you look at the numbers. This philosophy has never failed me. This statement should not be interpreted as 'brands do not matter' – rather brands become part of a bigger plan, and believe it or not, they will play an even bigger role.

Finally, trust that the spark will light when you realise what 'gap' you should be addressing. You will find that developing brands and campaigns that address these gaps will work brilliantly and growth becomes imminent. So every time you decide to make a turn, make the right turn using these pillars. Data doesn't lie.

ABOUT THE AUTHOR:
EDDIE MAALOUF

Partner

A 'venturer', self-starting, self-motivating, goal-oriented and impatient risk taker who always seeks revenue growth, Eddie is a Founder and Partner at ToughLove Advisors and the former Sr Vice President for Nokia Mobile Phones MEA.

Eddie carries 30 years of experience across multiple industries spanning more than 90 countries. A marketer by blood, he has been known to toy around with multiple expertise, from brand launches to operational development, to new market entries. He has a strong passion for aligning market opportunities with people and portfolio capabilities to deliver growth!

Eddie has worked for some of the largest brands in the region, operating in Telecom, FMCG, CPG, Professional Services and his own exited Start Up. A seasoned speaker in the MENA region and a former member of the Clinton Global Initiative (CGI) and the Young Arab Leaders UAE Chapter (YAL), he is currently a member of The Marketing Society.

Eddie speaks five languages and holds a Master's degree in international marketing as well as a BBA in Photojournalism and Advertising. He loves nothing more than a challenge for growth.

Promising Minds and Winning Hearts

TIM BURNELL

Lessons from UAE-origin global brands – In an era of increased competition, squeezed margins and proliferation of choices, how does a brand become beloved by its consumers?

THE DATING GAME

On my last blind date, my guest arrived full of interest in all the aspects of myself that I had carefully pitched and planted out there through mutual friends and online profiles. Sadly, the Tim Burnell that showed up that evening was feeling a little distracted, tired, and consequently forgetful of some of the elements that make a great get-together. Despite my best efforts at preparing, when it came to the actual date I failed to listen well, my body language was awkward, my storytelling felt tongue-tied and my mind was clearly elsewhere. Unsurprisingly, I recall neither living up to the billing nor being given a second chance.

Imagine then, a blind date with your own brand. What information have you seen or heard, and what are your expectations? Why are you interested, and what are you looking for?

What first impressions will you have, and what will you feel during the encounter? What thoughts might you take away? Will you be excited about a next date?

If dating your brand doesn't appeal as much as you hoped, then the themes covered here should prove useful in making it a more lovable proposition.

BRAND TALK, NO WALK

As marketers, we spend the majority of the time planning, crafting, and explaining our brand. We categorise it for every locale, segment, and persona. We justify its impact and try to manage the perception it creates. We constantly groom and tweak it based on a variety of research, performance data, critique and anecdotes. We proudly build communications around its principles, often specifically to justify the promises we make or, worse, sometimes to hide gaps and issues. We love to obsess over our brand's purpose, correctness, and relevance. We measure its real success based mainly on commercial returns, especially in the short term. We even use any engagement with our marketing as a proxy for our customers' actual relationship with our products and services.

These are mostly honourable considerations and actions, but they lack focus on the real moments of interaction. In a nutshell, we should be asking ourselves if we are fully managing the brand experience. The answer will almost certainly be no, because as marketers we can't physically deliver personal service at every touchpoint, even if we wanted to. However, we can take a much more active role in the design of the brand, and we can influence the product quality and multiple steps in the customer journey.

I am reminded of a colleague of mine, with responsibility for a huge catalogue of retail, gaming and entertainment offerings to travellers, who added his name and contact details to the product information that was part of the customer's core experience. He received thousands of personal messages, which he diligently used to refresh the catalogue monthly and achieve award-winning levels of customer satisfaction and a reputation for recognition and personalisation.

Despite this lovely example of a great practice, how often do we genuinely and as a matter of habit, dig further into the characteristics that make our brand a part of our lives – at least in the same way that we are so keen for our customers to? For marketers, there is huge benefit in stepping firmly into our customers' shoes to truly sample the intricacies, highs and lows of the experience and compare it to the promises we advertise. Moreover, if this immersion is coupled with a deep and smart analysis of customer feedback, particularly the unsolicited kind, we can learn much about any failings in delivery and outcome against the expectations we so passionately built up.

So, whether your business is purely commercial, 'not for profit' or somewhere in between, as a brand it will only grow to be meaningful, indispensable, and ideally even loved, when its promises are consistently and fully delivered during your customers' interactions and experiences with the various products and services ... time after time.

LEVERAGING YOUR BRAND

Have you ever taken time to reflect on why your brand isn't as important for people or desired as much as you believe it should be? Are you often surprised that only a small percentage of customers are aspiring to your premium offerings? Do you sometimes feel that your business operation falls short of the communicated proposition?

If the answers to these questions are yes then you are also likely to have faced poor net promoter scores, low consideration, limited engagement, and overall weak brand strength. At regular business review meetings, the question will inevitably arise: Is it the brand that is underperforming or the operation, the product, or the service delivery? For the marketing team who are running great campaigns on a strong brand platform, this signals either a disconnect with the customer or a failing in their experience. In short, the brand is not being fully leveraged and is not sufficiently influencing the business.

I have been fortunate enough to work for four of the strongest global brands with their home base in the UAE, namely Emirates, Dnata, FAB (First Abu Dhabi Bank) and Etihad. Each of these organisations has invested large amounts of resource in customer-centric processes and initiatives, building them into long-term strategies and maintaining a close watch over service delivery standards.

In this chapter, we will cover some real examples of what can work to best balance your brand's intent with its actual impact. We will look at important things to consider and do when building a brand that not only offers a platform to present your services to consumers but also enables your organisation to deliver an experience to match the bold promises communicated to customers and stakeholders in the business.

Let's call our theme 'brand promise and delivery reality'. It is highlighted in a variety of stories from Middle Eastern aviation and banking brands. These stories help to illustrate some key strategies, plans and actions required to successfully conceive, build, manage and nurture a brand that provides clear benefits and leverage to the business strategy and operation. This leads, in turn to designing and delivering an experience that exceeds expectation on the path we started down … to win hearts.

EVERYONE LOVES EMIRATES

Emirates is a well-respected but relatively young airline that has been riding waves of success, often leapfrogging its competitors, especially during times of crisis for the travel industry. It is regularly looking to elevate its reputation and position in the market whilst constantly aiming to strengthen its offering and prevent any chance of stagnating.

The story of Emirates' 'Hello Tomorrow' brand platform is a compelling one that shows the effect of a refresh on the existing highly recognised 'master brand'. It also highlights Emirates' ability to help take a great product and strategy to the next level, leveraging its marketing, communications and culture.

For this iteration of the brand in an evolving cycle of refreshes, the task was to reposition and distinguish the iconic airline company for high growth in a low-innovation market, while uniting a multi-cultural, multilingual global workforce of 60,000. Quite a big ask!

Simply put, the answer, a 'Hello Tomorrow' movement, was an open-armed greeting to our borderless world. It positioned Emirates as the first truly global airline, inspiring interconnectedness among world travellers.

The change to the Emirates brand platform that 'Hello Tomorrow' delivered worked beautifully and directly. It was a natural progression from the previous 'Keep Discovering' brand line and maintained the standard of showing the true excitement, anticipation and joy of travel in people's lives. These creative expressions were lauded for their impact, and the campaigns consistently drove awareness, interest and consideration to higher levels.

If we look under the bonnet to see the engine of this new brand development, we find dynamic data and behavioural insights combining with a crucially strong company vision and long-term understanding of customer needs. These elements came and stayed together to influence a brand that could build reputation, love, and expectation on top of an already great product and customer experience. This is a notably exceptional example of using a fresh look at insights – in this case, the enthusiasm for and proliferation of global travel as a life priority – to start a movement that gives purpose to an organisation's growth.

Strategically, Emirates had realised that a clear mandate to provide the best airline product experience 'door-to-door', based on service, comfort, convenience, entertainment and safety could be trusted to delight customers, and it is this that gives the brand the freedom to act with courage. Furthermore, even though the 'Hello Tomorrow' rebrand was conceived in a golden time for global travel, Emirates' single-minded and long-standing vision to be the largest and best airline had already given them the confidence to buck travel trends and take risks during downturns that reaped great benefit when the market bounced back. Let's not forget that this strong vision was shared by Dubai. For an airline that is the calling card of its home base, this is a huge strategic benefit.

There is much here to celebrate and imitate. Combining a clear vision and business strategy with insightful branding builds strong relationships with customers over time, adding to the organisations' confidence to innovate and take calculated risks that can have industry-changing impact. Henry Ford created a car based on such confidence to innovate, not the faster horse his customers asked for.

THE CMO'S INFLUENCE

Marketing is playing a big role in the trend of businesses seeking purpose, resetting their culture and improving their experience for all stakeholders. At the practical leadership level, there is a lot that the CMO or more appropriately, the Chief Marketing and Experience Officer, can do to create the environment for brands to thrive and achieve a more positive impact on the organisation and their customers.

This starts, very simply, with the design of the marketing team, which, in addition to the usual functional managers and media experts, should include product specialists, data and behavioural analysts and designers to shape the customer experience. Every member of the team will need to act like champions and ambassadors who can drive the required relationships internally across the business and constantly push for superior product and service delivery. It sounds straightforward, but the team set-up has a fundamental influence on all elements of the outputs directly influencing the customer journey. And as in any performance in the arts, entertainment or sport, this team must be both capable and dedicated to working together under a strong leader to deliver fully and punch above its weight in a time of resource constraints.

Culture-wise, the team requires strong traits – consistency, confidence, diversity, and business expertise to communicate credibly, both internally and externally. Moreover, a strong, charismatic, and courageous CMO will be able to react to the current climate of a global pandemic-influenced downturn, long-overdue championing of equality and mental health, digitally driven lifestyle norms, and the acceptance of a need to look after our planet.

In fact, beyond the foundation of product and service excellence, a focus on the community as much as on shareholders opens the door to creating a more emotional bond between organisations, customers and society, a bond based on meaningful themes such as diversity, sustainability, equality, and wellbeing, in addition to commercial performance.

This approach will win hearts and minds and is more likely to allow organisations to achieve real relevancy with what customers need, value, and engage with. It should see the championing of more innovation in markets that will be characterised by superfast disruption and very little continuity.

MARKETING-LED STRATEGY

Whilst CMOs can champion the environment to nurture both culture and brand to be more purposeful and relevant, there is a real overall business benefit in allowing revenue-generation strategies to predominate over cost management. It is tempting to let Finance, HR and Procurement teams lead decisions that shape operations and define customer offerings, leaving marketing and brand to package the product reactively. However, if we accept that marketing should understand the customer better than the rest of the organisation, then why not let it take the lead in generating market share and revenue performance through long-term superior customer propositions, rather than short-term, cost management strategies and restrictions in product quality and service?

Convincing the organisation of this requires tactics such as clear shared metrics, attribution models, direct return on marketing investment and performance dashboards highlighting Net Promoter Scores, customer engagement and brand health, and analysing the dependencies between them.

Also, great creativity should be at the centre of a content strategy that showcases the product, service, and customer benefits. The power of screens to create love for a brand means that consistently vibrant and engaging messages will be very effective. Of course, all communications, visual and digital experiences, interactions, and touchpoints have to match the brand promise. This great visual content will also be very powerful internally in training and immersing the organisation.

Where does all this leave us in our quest for love? As we have touched on, the real opportunities to create customer love come when organisations are strategically strong, aligned, consistent and dynamic. They understand that creating preference, loyalty and advocacy with real, useful, relevant, and satisfying offerings is not merely a promotional or commercial action. They believe that branding as a stamp, promise and reassurance that cannot be underdelivered will push the operation to optimise and the business to do better. They will ensure that customer-centric thinking creates a hub mentality that ensures all customer and user experiences meet the criteria for customer love.

The brand platforms created in such organisations can be true blueprints for the real relationship between your customer and your offer. Done well, this creates lovemarks, a term coined by Kevin Roberts at Saatchi & Saatchi, that is, brands that over a sustained period have transcended the transactional nature of the relationship to intimately become a part of customer thinking and living. Marketing teams are best placed to lead this.

REGIONAL BRAND INITIATIVES

Coming back to our regional bands, let's have a look at some specific examples of company initiatives to really drive customer sentiment improvements through improved product and service.

As part of the FAB's (First Abu Dhabi Banks) move to address clear indicators that customers felt service could be improved, the bank invested in a service training programme to instil top-level behaviours in all staff: front line, back-of-house, operational, business services, managerial and leadership. The programme was fully interactive, enabling staff to role-play service scenarios and learn from case studies of leading service providers in industries such as private health, luxury hotels and theme parks. The results were immediate in terms of understanding the gaps, building improvement plans and making customers happier.

At Dnata, the most significant rebrand embraced a one-team philosophy in evolving a legacy of 25 different brands to 'One Dnata' united by a single objective to provide the best ground support to the travel industry. At the heart of the programme was the development and implementation of customer- and people-first processes in what was a predominantly operational company. The culture was thus built from the inside out, enabling all its staff to work towards challenging targets for customer satisfaction with clarity and purpose. Recognition of success by any element of the team remains integral to One Dnata, where team spirit is at the heart of satisfying customers.

Again, back at Emirates they realised that the success of the aviation-leading business strategy and historically strong brand platforms would be enhanced by evolving their set of service values. The theme for developing these was to allow natural and nuanced differences in culture and character from over 150 nationalities to shine through – but underpinned by a clear set of service behaviour characteristics. This approach perfectly complemented the culture of Emirates, which was to be global in its operation not just its distribution. The result has charmed passengers and created memorable moments above and beyond the excellent levels of service.

Emirates also developed a hub for immersive training that authentically recreated environments for all types of customer interaction. Every member of staff was required to pass the training and thus become very aware of the real engine of the company's success … its commitment to a superior travel experience.

ETIHAD'S CHOICES

At Etihad, a transformation programme was implemented to control costs in a business model that had loyal customers used to and expecting remarkable service from a remarkable place, Abu Dhabi.

The programme had a clearly defined outcome and required a shared purpose to create the fastest route to staff alignment and engagement. A fundamental change to the business model and a changed customer proposition meant that the brand platform had to manage significant changes in customer experience and the resulting perceptions and changes to reputation.

In Etihad's case, the new brand platform, 'Choose Well', sought to position Etihad as a 'choice well made' and for all stakeholders, part of making the right choices in life. Naturally, this requires the full path to purchase and customer experience to reflect the elements of making good choices … i.e., good information, benefits versus the competition, ease of doing business, service standards, functional products, recognition, etc. And it forced the organisation to come together to focus collectively on delivering the desired outcome, of Etihad being the right choice in any situation it offered.

In terms of execution, this requires corporate, brand and internal messaging to be in sync, as well as all communications and campaigns to reflect the new customer offering. Performance-wise, because of the clarity and alignment in business strategy, culture, brand, and customer proposition, it should be clear what is driving any changes to NPS, engagement and brand health. This gives a great new baseline from which to drive longer-term customer love, but it is unusual to have such a blank sheet of paper on which to plan a company's future. Changes generally happen to different aspects of the organisation at different times.

In all the cited examples, the organisation had clear agreement that product quality and service, more than brand and communications, were the drivers of customer loyalty. This sounds like common sense, but the point to be made is that actually doing this thoroughly requires a focus much beyond the norm.

IT'S IMPORTANT TO ALIGN

We saw from these examples – One Dnata's singular culture, FAB's service initiatives, the elevation of Emirates' values to lifestyle partner levels, the transformational change to Etihad – that one essential aspect of winning customer and stakeholder hearts and minds is the strategic alignment between purpose, culture, operations, marketing, communications, product development and service delivery. An aligned, co-created, well-championed brand and communications platform will always stand a much better chance of driving the business to deliver a better customer experience than one being resisted or redesigned by specific parts of the organisation.

And of course, the complete business ecosystem needs to always be mindful of market trends and outside factors that will influence the relevance and competitiveness of any products and services. Brands that can add innovation and thrive on disruption will gain even more.

Naturally, this alignment is best derived from within. Beware the off-the-shelf solutions to shaping vision and mission, framing strategy, listing goals, creating values, and defining customer and employee propositions. These should be kept close to the heart of the organisation and tailor-made from the ground up to truly reflect something that can be delivered credibly.

FIVE TAKEAWAYS

It is useful to summarise some key takeaways from the themes and examples in this chapter to equip organisations to win customers' hearts and minds. These five are the most important to really help you focus on outcomes:

1. Add strong marketing analytics to a beautifully presented brand to influence senior leadership to be more

marketing-driven and revenue-focused in their planning. This can drive differentiation and competitive advantage, yet within reasonable cost and operational constraints.

2. Use the brand promise as a benchmark to push the business to constantly seek and be measured by high levels of customer satisfaction.

3. Build a superior product and service into the core purpose and vision. Align this across the whole of the organisation with clarity, coherence, and commitment.

4. Understand and measure all customer and stakeholder engagement with your product and service and react immediately to rectify any gap between the communicated and advertised promise and the experienced reality.

5. Create a culture that provides a helpful, sympathetic, and sophisticated environment in which to understand – along the path to purchase and the customer journey – what motivates customers to be loyal and admit the brand into their complex lives.

WHAT YOU CAN DO

Marketing and branding are comprehensively documented disciplines based on well-known elements and approaches, but I urge you here to diligently analyse how well-loved your business is and take deliberate and disruptive steps to ensure that you are fit for purpose and on your game to win hearts and minds.

There are no shortcuts to this. Please give some tough love to your organisation, your operation, your culture, your strategies, your plans and, of course, your products and services to see how well they are doing in the quest to be loved. That way the blind date will definitely not disappoint.

ABOUT THE AUTHOR:
TIM BURNELL

Partner

Tim is passionate about marketing, branding, communications, and Customer Experience. He has worked in energy, aviation, banking, and advertising for over 30 years.

Tim specialises in delivering business strategy, brand and culture programmes, organisational change, campaigns, corporate communications, Customer Experience and transformation initiatives for businesses with a global presence.

He grew his career in the UK and Africa with BP and Lowe before moving to the Middle East to take up leadership roles with Emirates, FAB and Etihad, latterly specialising in brand and experience transformation.

Tim is an active professional musician, blending learnings from performing and business in a collaborative, agile and positive, outcome-driven style.

He lives in London and Dubai.

Transform to stay in the game.

NAMRATA BALWANI

'EACH PART OF NATURE WANTS TO GO
ON WITH ITS OLD MOVEMENTS AND
REFUSES, SO FAR AS IT CAN, TO ADMIT
A RADICAL CHANGE AND PROGRESS,
BECAUSE THAT WOULD SUBJECT IT TO
SOMETHING HIGHER THAN ITSELF AND
DEPRIVE IT OF ITS SOVEREIGNTY IN ITS
OWN FIELD, ITS SEPARATE EMPIRE. IT IS THIS
THAT MAKES TRANSFORMATION SUCH A
LONG AND DIFFICULT PROCESS.'

— SRI AUROBINDO, BASES OF YOGA

We all wish for transformational situations in our lives. That magical moment when everything that we've wished for is suddenly true. Becoming the person that we always wanted to be – smarter, happier, thinner, fatter, richer, mindful, carefree. It could be anything. However, taking the actions to make a change is hard. Inertia plays a powerful role for many of us.

As difficult as this is for individuals, it is even harder for businesses. We have an inherent resistance to transformation, just as Sri Aurobindo said. But in our evolutionary history we've gone from once upon a time saying, 'If it ain't broke, don't fix it' to 'Move fast and break things', a philosophy that became cool when Mark Zuckerberg said it. The technology-driven business ecosystem compels many traditional organisations to go through Digital Transformation.

HOW IT STARTED

In 2005, when digital media in India was still new, when 'digital marketing' was still something to do with 'IT (Information Technology)', I took a leap of faith and co-founded a digital marketing agency in India; along with my fellow co-founder, and our primary investor. At the time, a digital marketing budget was an insignificant set of 0s. However, many digital agencies had already been founded. There was the sense that a great opportunity lay before us. It was a time when not even 2.5% of India's population were on the internet. Today, that number is almost 50%, second only to China, and higher than the population of the United States. The share of spending on digital media is slated to overtake TV in India very soon.

But those were the days of 'microsites' (a small website, of a few pages, typically built for ad campaigns, different from the 'corporate website' or the company's official website) and 'viral films' (mostly animated films designed to spread naturally amongst an audience because of their engaging nature), and Facebook itself was probably a year old. 'Digital media', once something to be handled by a different department in an ad agency, with its own language, has consistently changed over time to where we are today.

Marketing has moved from 'mass' (marketing to the widest possible customer base) to 'personalised' (using data to deliver brand messages targeted to an individual or a smaller group of prospective customers); from 'segments' (groups of customers created based on demographics, geography, psychographics and/or behavioural actions) to 'signals' (pieces of information consumers and businesses create through their everyday actions indicating they are potential customers, e.g., a transaction, an enquiry, or interest in a specific activity); from 'users' (typically, anyone who visits a website or an app) to 'consumers' (a person who purchases goods or services for their use).

We are in the age of the Immersive Economy, having just come through the Experience Economy.

That decade from 2005–2015 was one crazy rollercoaster ride. Building a start-up is exhilarating and agonising at the same time. Doing this as the digital medium itself is evolving, learning new things, adapting to changing technology, and keeping the agency ahead of the curve – it was like being on a treadmill that never stopped. We had a deep-seated desire to do great work that spoke for itself. We won new business. There were many leading brands we brought onto the digital medium for the first time. There were several digital ad campaigns we created that were ahead of their time.

In 2007, we had to create awareness about a telecom company's superior mobile network quality. Working with our resident 'creative genius' and a core team, we shot several high-quality videos. They were humorous 'studies' of people who were victims of an inferior mobile network, suffering from things like 'high decibel mobile disease' (a disease that makes you speak loudly because the person at the other end cannot hear you) or 'Signal Search Syndrome' (contorting yourself into weird positions in that one spot where you have mobile network coverage). Video, especially high-quality video shot for the digital medium, was a rarity then.

In 2009, as Twitter was increasingly becoming popular in India, we created a banner on MSN India (Microsoft's 'web portal' for news and entertainment as it was called then) that displayed live tweets in an AMA (Ask Me Anything) format, with the brand mascot of a leading Direct-To-Home service provider). This had never been done. Answering questions live on behalf of the mascot was our team, moderating and responding in real-time, with the tweets not only showing up on Twitter but also within the banner on one of the largest general websites of the time.

In 2010, we created a parenting community on social media for a leading life insurance brand – again a first for its time, and in the category of life insurance. We brought together experts in various fields to help parents with their questions and concerns. We even had parents run the social community for a week each month to create rich, genuine conversations.

At the heart of each of these was the desire to stay ahead of how consumers were using the digital medium and of their changing relationship with brands. I was very proud of the many team members who joined us and believed in the same vision. But I'll be honest; at the end of the decade (2015) I was exhausted. It was time to take a break and move on to other things.

CHANGE IS GOOD

I moved cities, continuing the quest of not getting too comfortable, forcing myself to adapt to new situations and newer challenges. Joining Ogilvy, an iconic, global leader in creative, brand and strategic planning was an exciting move for me. I loved my stint there, but two years later, it was time for a change again. This time, I also changed countries. My attraction to this new role came from the opportunity to understand a different region, the Middle East, and to work for a company instead of an agency. Both were new experiences for me. Changing jobs and changing countries at the same time is not easy!

I moved to Dubai to set the digital roadmap for a large retail and hospitality company and to move marketing into an omnichannel approach, giving customers a seamless experience, irrespective of them shopping offline or online. Setting a digital transformation roadmap for businesses in different industries (involving the integration of digital technology into a business, changing how value is delivered to customers) required understanding consumer habits, customer journeys (the full experience of a customer interacting with a brand and purchasing a product or service), company operations, revenue goals, operational efficiencies and much more.

But I could see that many departments functioned independently in the organisation, and there was inertia in sharing valuable customer data because everyone was in their silo. The biggest challenge facing organisations that want to transform is this disconnected way of working, with teams having different objectives. I knew that setting this digital transformation roadmap required the organisation to understand their customer, whether they were offline (in a store) or online.

Understanding the consumer is paramount, and a Single Customer View (SCV) enables that. An SCV is simply a way to gather all the data related to a particular customer's interactions (for example, whether they visited the site, redeemed loyalty points, purchased in a store, etc.) and create a single record so that disparate data sets can be matched as being the actions of one customer. This is important: if a company can better understand their customers, every department (sales, marketing, customer service, operations) can orient itself to become more relevant to them. Customers can be given what they really want because companies get better at predicting what it is.

Without an SCV, executing a marketing strategy for a seamless experience on any marketing channel would be hard. For example, without a history of their transactions available in real-time, we cannot make suggestions on what else a customer purchasing something in-store might want or need. We see this sort of recommendation all the time online, but it is much harder to achieve in-store if the customer data is not already unified and available.

I championed a Digital Transformation journey that meant crafting the right Customer Experience (CX) – the customers' entirety of experiences with a brand through any point of contact. It defined how we want to capture, store, manage and process Customer Data using technology to enable delivery across departments. This naturally led to the next step, a data and analytics setup to ensure that we drove incremental revenue through better customer acquisition (acquiring new customers) and customer retention (retaining existing customers) strategies.

CHANGE BRINGS RESULTS

In one of our businesses, the journey from a new customer enquiry to getting the customer to complete the purchase was broken. We knew this because we were not tracking details such as the channel from which the customer placed the enquiry, whether the customer purchased a subscription, how much they spent, and so on. It took manual effort to get all this data together; we had to obtain reports from diverse departments – marketing, sales, operations, customer service, finance – which slowed down our understanding of whether our marketing and sales efforts were effective. Manual inputs by teams were also prone to error.

We had behavioural data coming in through third-party apps, but they were not integrated with our transactions data. This meant that not only did we not know our customers in-depth, but that our speed to execute campaigns through the customer lifecycle was slow as well. These campaigns were bursts of static output with no dynamic personalisation. Dynamic personalisation is content that adapts to each customer based on their behaviour, so that what we show customers nudges them towards a purchase. An example would be showing you the exact contents of that shopping cart you abandoned, on a different channel, with an appropriate message.

If you are interested in joining a gym for yoga, for example, showing you the yoga facilities, or giving more information about the yoga instructors will be more effective than showing you photos of the weights area. You will more likely accept emails related to yoga facilities than plain old 'sign-up to the gym' emails. Using technology can help automate the provision of relevant communication to millions of customers.

Not having this customer data integration also meant that we couldn't meaningfully attempt to predict when a customer would leave the gym, nor could we improve how we retained customers, which requires data based on actual behavioural identifiers – for example, which parts of the gym did they use, what interested them, what were their motivations and how did these change on the journey to fitness.

We needed a better Marketing Technology solution to track how effective our efforts were – for example, in reducing the cost of acquiring a new customer or identifying the more profitable customer segments or increasing the total revenue that we earned over time from a customer. All these changes had significant, tangible impacts on revenue. Of course, one can implement everything correctly and then find that employees don't use these new systems! Transformation is a never-ending journey.

I have most often seen initiatives falter at the crucial moment when programmes kick off. The team, usually already overworked, has no time to spend on correctly implementing the training or utilising all the features of a tool. They are wary of what can be achieved by changing their ways of working. The temptation is to go back to the old way. A few days of training are not sufficient to change behaviour. It requires re-wiring methods of working. To test and fail does not come as easily to traditional businesses as it does to nimbler start-ups. This needs to be countered with consistent communication of the larger vision, regular checks on the quality of usage and whether there has been a change in the key metrics that measure performance.

CHANGE IS HARD

All this sounds very logical and linear however implementing a digital transformation project is anything but. It can be messy. I remember one occasion when I needed nine signatures on a piece of paper to enable some activities. How ironic is that for a digital transformation project? The idea that a top-down approach can just be implemented is a fallacy. Every department must be co-opted into the process.

Let's face it, people have tremendous inertia in changing how they do their daily job. If digital transformation efforts reduce manual input, automate many parts of the business operations and effectively free up time to do more strategic thinking, people need to be skilled for that. Departments need to work together and understand that data transparency is good for the achievement of the larger vision.

Take the role of Marketing. Marketing, Digital, Data, and Tech are all interconnected. Today's Marketing Leader must wear many hats.

The Brand Hat

The Data Hat

The Tech Hat

The Revenue Hat

The People Influencer Hat

The Sales Hat

The Distribution Hat

The Finance Hat.

Without understanding the dynamics and priorities of each department, it's hard to change how the organisation approaches Marketing. Customer Experience is rooted in employee experience.

But there is also the danger of going from one extreme – of disconnected experiences – to the other extreme: too *much* communication with customers. Many organisations today grapple with too much data, from too many sources, that are not linked in a discernible way; yet such data are still used for taking decisions. The idea that all data are useful is a fallacy. To be useful, data need to be linked, validated, and analysed. In the quest to always 'nudge' the customer towards a purchase, marketing automation technology is often over-used. When you jump to marketing automation programmes before understanding customer needs, you may not even understand the validity of the data that you gather. The marketing automation programme can end up becoming a nag.

Many things can disrupt a customer's path to purchase:

- Sometimes they don't want to complete that purchase right that minute.
- Sometimes the cost of delivery is as high as the product, but they only find that out right at the end.
- Sometimes it is an impulse, but they decide to control it.
- Sometimes they felt like they needed to do more research.
- Sometimes they receive a phone call.
- Sometimes the ad is great, but the page it leads them to has nothing related to the ad.

- Sometimes the promo code doesn't work anymore.
- Sometimes they have already completed the purchase.
- Sometimes they've been told the same thing on three other channels already.
- Sometimes the brand is just boring.

It is important to build the brand, understand the customer journey, eliminate breaks and gaps in data flow, make communication strategy creative and consistent, consider the quality of messaging over quantity, identify the best channels, and send relevant communication, instead of blasting email messages.

Data is critical, but the blind collection of data with no discernible difference to a customer is meaningless. Data saturation has a very real impact on Customer Experience. The better approach is to start with the core business objectives and the key questions to be answered – and then go seek out the right data. Collecting data just because it's there to be collected does not help. Always know the 'why' and the 'what'. Why do you need data and what purpose will data serve?

One often hears that if only it could buy many tools, the company would attain digital nirvana – data-driven business decisions that bring in additional revenue and make customers happy. Does a company need to buy a CDP (Customer Data Platform), a DMP (Data Management Platform), a CRM (Customer Relationship Management system), a Marketing Automation tool and look at Business Intelligence (BI), Machine Learning (ML) and Artificial Intelligence (AI)?

TRANSFORM TO STAY IN THE GAME.

Companies need some basics to get started, sure, but if one doesn't already have a strategy and the right thinking embedded in the organisation, such tools alone are not going to help.

Before one starts buying and building, one needs to think about what role that data is going to play for Customer Experience, what problems are to be solved, what can be done with currently available data, what is preventing effective use of the current data, who is the sponsor and who is the champion for such an initiative, what skill-sets are needed to derive full value from such investments, and what is the governance plan.

DIGITAL TRANSFORMATION REQUIRES A HOLISTIC APPROACH.

Thinking about **People Transformation** is as important as thinking about business transformation – people as both customers and employees. It's not about technology alone. There are plenty of tools available, but without planning for and measuring the impact on people, business transformation cannot be successful. It's not only about the corporate office, the leadership team, or key people. Success comes from involving frontline staff who interact with customers every day. If they don't understand the organisational vision, none of this will be possible.

Go Big or Go Home because focusing on just one area of business or one department will get limited results. When thinking about the customer journey, realise that the entire company is involved in it in different ways. Reshaping only a part of a business will lead to broken experiences. It's far more effective to think about transformation across the company.

Adaptability is critical, as there will come a time in any implementation design that requires rethinking roles or process flows or team structures. It might take a year to implement change, but that year will bring further changes – in the way customers interact and the way competitors do business. That's why agile forms of collaborative working are so important.

Don't think of data and analytics as an outcome, but rather as part of the objective. It's important to think about what metrics are important for various stakeholders. This may evolve, but there needs to be a starting point so that the metrics and measurements contribute to KPIs across departments.

FIVE PILLARS OF DIGITAL TRANSFORMATION AT TOUGHLOVE

Our TOUGHLOVE Digital Transformation & Business Innovation Practice is built on five pillars:

Customer Experience

A well-researched customer journey will clearly demonstrate which areas need transformation and why. The starting point in transformation is the customer. Insight into what customers want and how those wants lead to loyalty will determine the transformation areas, e.g., improvement in productivity, better customer service, reshaping the entire journey, speed to market, and D2C initiatives. Linking the objectives to business outcomes; websites, apps, marketing on digital platforms; content, search, commerce, customer service – everything is integrated to provide a complete experience.

Data & Analytics

Not only data scientists but people across the organisation need to be comfortable with data; they need to understand that analytics begin with asking the right questions. What can you do with the data that you have now? What is preventing you from effectively using current data? What is your ideal single view of the customer? How will decision-making change because of investing in data?

Tools & Technology

Technology could entail modernising your legacy architecture or moving from on-premise to the cloud, for example. Tools help organisations connect with customers at every stage of the funnel to help them navigate the purchase journey. This has led to a strong need for organisations to assimilate different tools into a custom stack. When looking at tools, we assess the current data and tech maturity to recommend the right solutions and potential partners to implement the vision.

Innovation & Agility

Innovation and Agility are the cornerstones of delivering differentiating and customer-obsessed business outcomes. Customer centricity is first and foremost a mindset. We work with organisations to enable moving from a project-centric approach to a product-centric approach. In a product-centric approach, products are supported by dedicated teams that include product managers, designers and developers who own the delivery of features that deliver on objectives and key results.

People & Culture

The culture in any organisation is critical; it determines the way of life of a group of people: the behaviours, beliefs, values, and symbols they accept, generally without thinking about them, and that are passed along by communication and imitation from one generation to the next. Transformation requires building new muscle memory. Are capabilities continually enhanced? Is there a stronger adoption of technology that directly impacts day-to-day work? All of this is important to understand.

The purpose of digital transformation is to change how a company provides value to its customers through technology. A clear road map of how to provide that value and how to generate revenue from it makes all the difference. Without alignment on what adding value means and how it is measured will mean, it will be harder to prove that transformation is effective.

Once again, I believe that the idea of transformation must be built as a kind of muscle memory. There will never be a time to stop. Evolution, by nature, requires understanding the changes in consumer behaviour. Innovating to stay in step with change, developing new business lines and using data effectively to drive growth are all essential. Transformation may be long and difficult, but the only other option is death.

Today, the younger generations do not visit Google as their first stop to searching for information. They start with social media. What then is the future of the website? Or of Search Engine efforts in Marketing? How do we enable brand *discovery* on social feeds, and not just brand experiences? What technology shall we use to deploy and monitor content and what metrics do we use for measuring effectiveness? Transformation, as always, is constant.

'CHANGE IS INEVITABLE.
GROWTH IS OPTIONAL.'

– JOHN C. MAXWELL

Has this inspired you to challenge the status quo in your organisation? No pain, no gain! I find that to be true, whether your transformation is personal or professional. Let's return to what Sri Aurobindo said: 'Each part of nature wants to go on with its old movements'. But assessing your organisation's current state and using the five pillars mentioned above to create your holistic Digital Transformation plan should give you some impetus to begin this process.

Companies must be open to transformation to continue to be relevant to customers and to find sustainable sources of revenue. Is your organisation prepared for Digital Transformation? If not, to borrow a famous piece of movie dialogue, 'Give me a call. I'll fly with you.'

ABOUT THE AUTHOR:
NAMRATA BALWANI

Partner

With more than two decades of experience in India and the Middle East, Namrata loves bringing together business, marketing, data, and technology.

Her passion for digital led her to co-found an independent digital marketing agency in India before she turned 30. Within five years, it was voted as being among the Top Digital Marketing Agencies and won multiple industry awards for path-breaking work. She then led a unit of OgilvyOne in India as SVP.

She moved to the Landmark Group, headquartered in Dubai, to lead digital marketing, digital transformation, and customer analytics for Landmark Hospitality for the MENA region.

She is now passionate about sharing her knowledge and experience as a consultant. She has also served as Adjunct Faculty at Middlesex University, Dubai, and is currently a member of the MMA MarTech Council.

At TOUGHLOVE, Namrata leads Digital Transformation and Business Innovation Practice, and she believes that true transformation comes from a holistic approach encompassing customers, employees, data, and technology. When she is not working, you'll find her hiking, running, or reading.

Innovate Or Die!

Your Key to Survival in an Ever-Changing World

MOHAMED AL TAJER

Have you ever wondered why the so-called 'Hot' companies in most of the global brands' ranking keep changing their seats? Because it's too 'hot' to keep if you are sitting on your 'ass'!

But let's start with the definition of innovation. What is it? In simple terms, it's 'Doing new things ... or doing things in a new way'. Another definition is transforming great ideas into reality. In a recent study, 84% of top executives said they have innovation as their top priority, while only 6% said they were happy with their outcomes. Now that's a huge discrepancy.

For the past 20 years or so I've been following these rankings across multiple indices and have seen the rise and fall of many companies. In the past, it used to take years to topple a brand or a company from its high ranking, but the pace has accelerated so much that it can happen within a few years only – not more than the fingers in one of your hands to leave the charts forever!

But why? Why are the likes of Nokia no longer there? I remember when my dream was to move from FMCG companies to

technology companies because I felt they were the future …
and my favourite was Nokia. Here we go, it's confession time!
Yes, I wanted to join Nokia. That was in the early 2000s.

Back in the late '90s and early 2000s, I used to also admire
Pharma companies for putting one-third of their budget into
Research and Development. I still remember reading that a
pharmaceutical company could spend one billion dollars on
developing a drug; that journey could take up to 10 years,
with all the testing and approvals from food and drug admin-
istrators, and yet it might turn into a failure at year nine!
Novartis was at the top of their game then, and yes, I wanted
to work for them too.

I am also old enough to remember the jokes we used to hear
from other 'petrol head' kids about Korean cars. A cousin of
mine who used to be a taxi driver bought a Hyundai Stellar
in the mid-80s and everyone around him said 'why?'. They
were cheap and untested cars in our region. Was it fit to be a
workhorse as a taxi? I must say, I liked that car; it was larger
than its competitors, the Toyotas and Nissans of the time,
and it looked different. When I look at Hyundai cars, I can
see where they were and where they are now. When I was
studying Industrial Engineering, one of my charismatic pro-
fessors told us that in South Korea they hung billboards at
their factories saying, 'Export or Die'. He would ask us questions, like why does a ton of steel cost X, but when it goes to
Switzerland and they make Rolexes out of it, the value of the
same ton of steel goes up by 1000x at least?

Have you heard about Kaizen? In its simplest and briefest definitions, Kaizen means 'Continuous Improvement' in Japanese. At university again, I thought 'Kaizen' would be the answer to anything. This continued with me well into the early part of my career ... until I realised that it was not about bringing huge results in one go. It was about making incremental improvements, as the name suggested.

I remember when I was a brand manager of beverages at Unilever; we were 'trying' to 'innovate' the tea category, but we were 'afraid' of getting it wrong! That's because it was one of the most profitable categories in the company, and we worried about what the consumer would think about it. So, we went with small incremental enhancements. And the result? In 2021, the company decided to sell the whole category because, frankly speaking, they'd lost the plot. They had not innovated enough – they were not daring enough. It's sad to see it go.

These examples have made me decide always to embrace 'innovation' as a way of life ... as my life!

By the end of this chapter, I hope you will see innovation in the right way, unlike most businesspeople, who see it as a box they need to tick on the go. Those who think of it only in those terms usually see their brands and companies go into obscurity. Tough? Yes, but that's the tough love you might need to hear from me, both for your organisation and yourself. If you do, my job is done!

NO URGENCY!

I hate to see it when 'innovation' is called for in the last hour. When an organisation is struggling, management hurries to assemble teams to see what they can do, and the outcome is almost always implementing short-term fixes. Why? Because they don't have the money, the resources, or the time to do it properly. Or all of the above. This is where companies with complacent cultures suffer. They are too relaxed. Remember the frog in the pot of slowly boiling water, staying until he cooks? But the frog you've put on a hot pan jumps immediately because it's burning hot and he 'feels' it! Now, which frog do you want to be?

Now let me tell you why some organisations are good at innovation and why others get it wrong even if their intentions are good.

CULTURE

It's mostly the 'unwritten rules' that an organisation follows. Why unwritten? Because I have seen that statements of mission and vision are just framed and hung in boardrooms and not in employees' minds. Yes, it's that simple.

I've seen 'toxic' cultures put policies in place that protect the 'bad' and question the 'good'. Sometimes, it makes no sense to try to redesign a company culture, because they have stage-four cancer and nothing can be done except to pray for a miracle. Unfortunately, miracles don't happen as much as they used to. It's better to shut them down and start afresh with a new set of people you hand-pick.

But why, when organisations are doing well, is innovation not a priority? Because innovation is hard work, and when revenues are coming easily, no one wants to work hard; that's human nature. Let me take you back to kindergarten and the story of the Ant and the Grasshopper. The ant worked hard all spring and summer to collect food for the winter when there was plenty of it. The grasshopper saw there was plenty of food and thought that winter was far off in time, so why work hard? We all know what happened in the end. Nothing beats honest hard work, and I'm sure now you will go back down memory lane to figure out who from your class was an ant and who was a grasshopper!

INNOVATION DEPT, AKA R&D

To date, companies have had Research and Development departments responsible for new products and services. While this might work for some companies, it has failed in many others. I was part of an organisation with a Strategy Department … and guess what, they were just paper collectors and movers. They came to the planning cycle every year to ask us about our new initiatives. What? We had our plans but, again, 'Strategy Department' what was your job?

The organisation of 'innovation' should not be based on tenure or hierarchy over contribution and sound judgment and a bit of courage.

You see, Innovation is very fluid by nature, and you need that so you can always try new things and experiment. Established organisations are built for efficiencies and economies of scale and scaling up tried and tested methods. They have set processes concerning how to do it, and they discourage deviation from those processes and practices. Having design studios or separate teams carved out might be a better solution at least for now.

You see, success is not always planned. Many times it happens by accident and sheer luck. A long time ago I read a book about Social Backwardness and it had a very interesting sentence on the first page. It went something like this: In a 'System', there is chaos and in 'Chaos' there is a system.

THE FAMILY

I still remember when Wrigley wanted to transform its business from a single product to include other areas. They gathered the leaders of all functions to take us through a journey of transformation. They created a 'movement' within the organisation. It all started with the CEO and his team. Rarely have I seen the C-Suite *all* aligned to achieve that mission. Do you remember that janitor who said to the Nasa scientist that he wanted to land a man on the moon? Well at Wrigley, we did land on the moon! When our R&D (and it was a proper R&D) showed us the products they've created, we were positively stunned. They were *better* than the established brands out there! We transformed in a very short period. Wrigley remains one of the best companies I've worked for, and I have huge respect for them. This was because we had the right ecosystem for us to thrive. On my first day at Wrigley, everyone was talking passionately about the Wrigley family, the owners of the business. That concept of 'family' included all the employees, irrespective of their backgrounds, functions, tenure, geography, etc.

I remember that the late Mr Wrigley Sr used to tour all his operating businesses across the globe and meet the employees face to face. He was kind, respectful, and humble, besides being an astute businessman. He was passionate about what he did and the people he hired. We had a ritual at Wrigley whenever we are about to embark on a risky project. We all asked ourselves this question: What would Mr Wrigley Sr say about this? It was still practised long after he passed away. I've never seen that sense of family in any of the other companies I've worked for.

Of course, I have also seen other cultures and other bosses who perceived anything related to doing things differently, or investing in innovation, as a waste of time and company resources. My advice to those who work under such people is to run as if from the plague! Others will welcome your talent.

BE THE CHANGE YOU WANT TO SEE IN THIS WORLD

You can't change anyone before you change yourself, and that requires a lot of courage and continuous soul searching. A lot of us are good critics of others but not of ourselves. They say that nothing changes by changing nothing. If you want to improve anything, start with yourself. Being a good listener is a start. Embracing others and being empathetic are key.

This also can be a mindset! Back in 2010, I attended a seminar with Fredrick Haran in which he discussed research about the most innovative nations. People from these countries were asked to give a score on how innovative they were. To everybody's surprise, South Koreans gave themselves the lowest score globally. We're talking about the country that gave us Samsung, LG, Hyundai, KIA, and many more great companies. Fredrick said that the reason for this was that South Korea was thought of as a 'third-world' country. They felt they have to do more to become a 'first-world' one. This is what made 'Export or Die' a motto for all South Koreans … make sense?

CREATING A MOVEMENT

Start with yourself and your team. Allocate a small budget and test. That's right, no big strategies or frameworks, just a small budget. Let the team know they can use it and just sail. That's the quickest way to launch an innovation program.

But there is a catch: in very well-organised companies, it does not work all the time, because there are processes and gate-keepers and many other hurdles to clear before you can start something even simple and small.

You see, organisations are built around compliance and conforming to certain rules. Otherwise, it's chaos. Snowballing is the key to overcoming such situations.

HIRE FOR INNOVATION

In large organisations, people are hired for execution, not innovation. But what if all your employees were innovating? How about that? Could it be a dream? No, on the contrary. If you are in the hospitality industry, for example, whether you are front-facing or not, you should have customer empathy within you; that is a must! This is why some hotels and restaurants are better than others. When they hire, say, an accountant, they also check if he has the basics of the serving industry. Everyone is a servant – serving colleagues before the end customer.

I remember reading an article many years back while flying on a British Airways flight. It was in the inflight magazine and was about an air hostess of the famous Concorde. And believe me, the cockpit and cabin crews on these fine birds were the best of the best. She was in her forties and was asked if there were many younger and 'prettier' women that the Concorde guest might prefer to see. I still remember her answer. She said that passengers flying the Concorde were there for the exceptional experience and service – and that comes only from exceptionally experienced cabin crew. End of story.

If there is one lesson to take from this chapter, it is to hire for innovation, always.

START SMALL AND BUILD ON IT

One time, I thought the organisation I was working for would give us a budget to use for coffee-time projects. I was wrong. I learned the buck stops here. So, I took charge and started to carve out a small budget for me and my team to test new things – and to protect them from the likes of the accountants and others who would ask for ROIs and things like that. This operation was undertaken purely to discover new things; I was clear that we needed to fail in order to succeed. No KPIs, no conditions, just the freedom to explore, with me shielding my team from unwelcome criticism. Guess what? The outcomes we had helped the business in many ways, and I learned to give voice to the voiceless in the team. There were a lot of smart people; I just need to make sure they were heard. Those who are shy and don't usually speak up – given the chance – will come up with ideas that will blow your mind. And I was blown away! Remember, small steps … Rome was not built in a day.

If your organisation is not supportive of innovation, or just pays it lip service, you'll need to carve out a piece of the organisation that obeys different rules and different processes, and that has small and nimbler cross-functional teams. A great example that comes to mind is 'skunk works'.

A skunk works project is one developed by a relatively small and loosely structured group of people. They research and develop, often with a very large degree of autonomy, primarily for the sake of radical innovation. The term originated with Lockheed's World War II Skunk Works project but typically refers to technology projects developed in semi-secrecy, such as Google X Lab. Other famous skunk works were Microsoft Research, special teams at Boeing, and the lab of about 50 people established by Steve Jobs to develop the Macintosh computer, located behind the Good Earth Restaurant in Cupertino.

At Unilever, when we were very serious about R&D projects, be it for the tea business or hair care, we used to have code names, and not even your neighbour at the office would know about it. This was laughed at when I joined the banking industry, where I found that everyone knew everything about the new products pipeline. How about some confidentiality here, please?

You will find that 'good' companies exit 'great' people because 'good' is the enemy of 'great'. Those 'good companies' now are the first frog who is very comfortable with the warmth of the pot.

LOOKING OUTSIDE

If you keep your customer at the centre of what you do and also look at what your counterparts are doing, you may be surprised to find that a lot of innovative ideas come from industries outside your own. When I moved to banking in 2006, after working briefly in the airline industry, I realised that in banking the customer is just a series of transactions, just a number! That was when customers were yearning for human and almost hotel- or hospitality-style experiences. They wanted to trust the bank and the banker, especially after the financial crisis of 2008–2010. I had to look back and tap my airlines and FMCG experience to make the customer a 'king' in Banking. This was a long but worthwhile exercise in a very rigid and pompous industry – at least at that time.

BETTER IS THE ENEMY OF NEW

New always takes time and comes with failures. Making things better requires less energy, and you are not really sticking your neck out too much – so you can keep your job! A good example was Lipton Tea, where the team was just tinkering with the product and the brand in small, incremental improvements – until it shrank and was sold to another company, quite recently. Having courage and taking bold moves is at the heart of the innovation process.

SUSTAINING INNOVATION VS DISRUPTIVE INNOVATION

The first one is mastered by big organisations while the second is mastered by the smaller unknown contenders. In my opinion, you need both at any organisation. But how do you manage that?

Large companies are not good at catering to small niches because of their heavy cost structure and established policies and processes. The job of Disruptive Innovation should be given to a 'spin-off' with a lower cost structure and more freedom.

This is exactly what has happened with fintech start-ups eating the 'payments' space away from established banks and payment associations. They have leveraged the fact that banks are not interested in small ticket payments and remittances for mass customers. They do it faster and cheaper. I remember when I used to discuss this with bankers; I always got the same answer, that there were not enough margins in this business. The rest is history. You see, large companies execute known business models, but start-ups search for new business models.

HOW CLEAR IS YOUR VISION?

You will be surprised sometimes by how each employee can have a different version of your vision. If you don't believe me, just bring together a bunch of employees from different departments (preferably ones who don't interact with each other), ask each one, 'What is the vision of your company?' and prepare to be amazed by the answers. I've been in that situation before. The Germans say that if you point one finger at me, three fingers point back at you, but I still hold that the leader or CEO is responsible – for not making the vision clear, not living it him or herself, and doing by example. I've worked with seniors who locked themselves all day in their offices and avoided interacting with their teams. How can you be a role model if your team can't see you, let alone speak to you? These were smart bosses, but they were terrible when it came to people management, let alone motivation. Many times, of course, the 'vision' is so bland and clichéd that no one even remembers what you stand for. So don't be surprised if your team does not do what you want them to do.

In conclusion, I would like to leave you with a few thoughts to ponder:

- Innovation requires foresight, bravery, and a sense of urgency – even when the business is doing great, in fact, more so if you are doing great.
- Innovation is an 'investment' and not a 'cost', but if you insist, treat it as the 'cost' to learn. That should make your CFO happy!
- 'Disruptive innovations' don't usually come from 'incremental improvements'. At least not if you want a standing ovation for it.
- To have what we call an 'Innovations Culture', you must institutionalise it across the board, and everyone has to

buy and believe it. You need to walk the talk at every level.

- Great products and services don't usually happen by accident! They are a result of a complete system.
- Hire for innovation (at least some), that is, people with 'innovative' mindsets. You will need a team of collaborators, promoters, etc. They will help you in creating the *movement.*
- Start *now* ... don't wait to perfect it!

Now, I know this be a daunting task for many, but we at ToughLove Advisors can help you in taking these steps and creating a culture of innovation.

Congratulations to you who have made it this far. I'll leave you with two questions:

'What will you do first thing tomorrow when you go to your office? What will you change?'

ABOUT THE AUTHOR: MOHAMED AL TAJER

Partner

Mohamed Al Tajer is fascinated by ideas and possesses an ability to find connections between seemingly disparate phenomena. He has a reputation for innovative thinking and seeks to transform something strong into something superb! His driving philosophy is that everyone has the right to receive knowledge!

Mohamed is a board member, entrepreneur, and mentor.

He is a leader with thirty years of global experience, including in Fortune 500 companies, in Financial Services, Fast-Moving Consumer Goods, Airlines, Retail, Fintech, Consulting & Business Mentoring. He has worked and lived in the UK, Germany, Saudi Arabia, UAE, Kuwait, and Bahrain. He has led large teams across multiple continents, in Europe, The Middle East, Africa, and Asia, in over 45 countries. Companies Mohamed has worked for include Citi, Wrigley, Unilever, Coca-Cola, National Bank of Qatar, National Bank of Kuwait, Majid Al Futtaim, Gulf Air and Mirathi among others.

Mohamed is,

Chairman of the Advisory Board of the CMO Council

Board Member of Mirathi.io

Co-Founder of TOUGHLOVE Advisors

Fellow of the Chartered Institute of Marketing, CIM, United Kingdom

Ranked one of '50 Most Talented CMOs' – World Marketing Summit, a Philip Kotler initiative.

CONCLUSION

Congratulations, if you have made it this far it means you enjoyed reading some of these chapters, perhaps scanned others, and hopefully became inspired and learnt a thing or two about topics that interests you.

This book intends to share our 250 years of combined experience and learnings from our successes and failures and to inspire you to reflect on what you can do better to grow both personally and professionally.

In this book, we have covered many real-life experiences, personal stories and examples about critical topics which impact organisations.

All the authors of this book are partners at a new-age advisory firm called TOUGHLOVE Advisors, which was born from an insight that traditional consulting models could be improved to better serve the needs of underserved businesses, such as small and medium enterprises (SMEs) and family-owned companies.

We call our approach the 'Tough Love Way', because it delivers wisdom in a courageous, transparent, and compassionate way, as if from a trusted friend or mentor who has insights, experience and knowledge from having been there and done it.

If you are not the sensitive type and wish to speak to any of our partners for some Tough Love advice or support with your business and growth challenges, the most effective way to reach us is:

Contact@toughloveadvisors.com

NOTES

www.ingramcontent.com/pod-product-compliance
Lightning Source LLC
Chambersburg PA
CBHW030514210326
41597CB00013B/905